Your Body

Childcraft

1990 Edition
Childcraft
3rd Reprint

Copyright © 1987 by World Book, Inc.
World Book House
77 Mount Ephraim
Tunbridge Wells
Kent TN4 8AZ, UK.

Portions of the text and certain illustrations previously
published under the title of **Childcraft** — The How and
Why Library.
Copyright © 1985, USA by World Book, Inc.
Merchandise Mart Plaza, Chicago, Illinois 60654, USA.
International Copyright © 1985 by World Book, Inc.

Printed in the USA.

ISBN 0-7166-6004-0

World Book (Australia) Pty. Ltd.
World Book House
71-73 Lithgow Street
St. Leonards
New South Wales 2065.

D/HI

Volume 5

Your
Body

World Book, Inc.
a Scott Fetzer company
Chicago London Sydney
Toronto

Contents

All about you!

Millions of children live in the world. But not one of those children is exactly like you.

The outside of you doesn't look exactly like anyone else. Your fingerprints and footprints are different from everyone else's. You smell different too. Because you have your own special scent, you can send a letter to your dog when you are away from home. You wipe your face and hands with a tissue, then fold it, put it in an envelope and post it. Your dog will know you sent the letter to him when he sniffs the tissue, because no one else has a scent exactly like yours.

The way you think and feel is special to you too. You have thoughts and feelings that are yours alone.

So on the outside and the inside you're special. There's only one of you in the whole world.

All the pages in this book tell you something about yourself – from the top of your head to the tips of your toes.

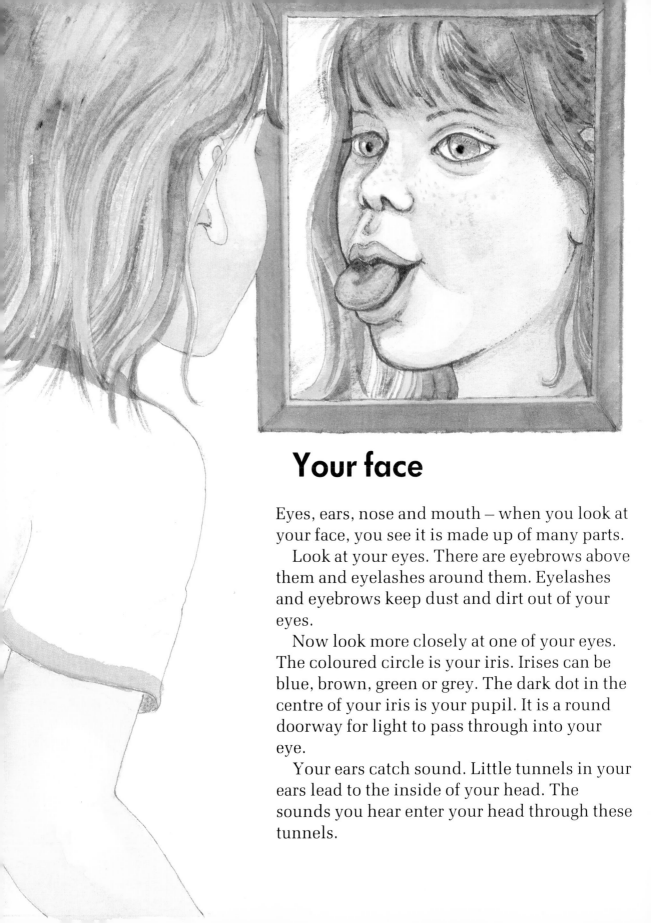

Your face

Eyes, ears, nose and mouth – when you look at your face, you see it is made up of many parts.

Look at your eyes. There are eyebrows above them and eyelashes around them. Eyelashes and eyebrows keep dust and dirt out of your eyes.

Now look more closely at one of your eyes. The coloured circle is your iris. Irises can be blue, brown, green or grey. The dark dot in the centre of your iris is your pupil. It is a round doorway for light to pass through into your eye.

Your ears catch sound. Little tunnels in your ears lead to the inside of your head. The sounds you hear enter your head through these tunnels.

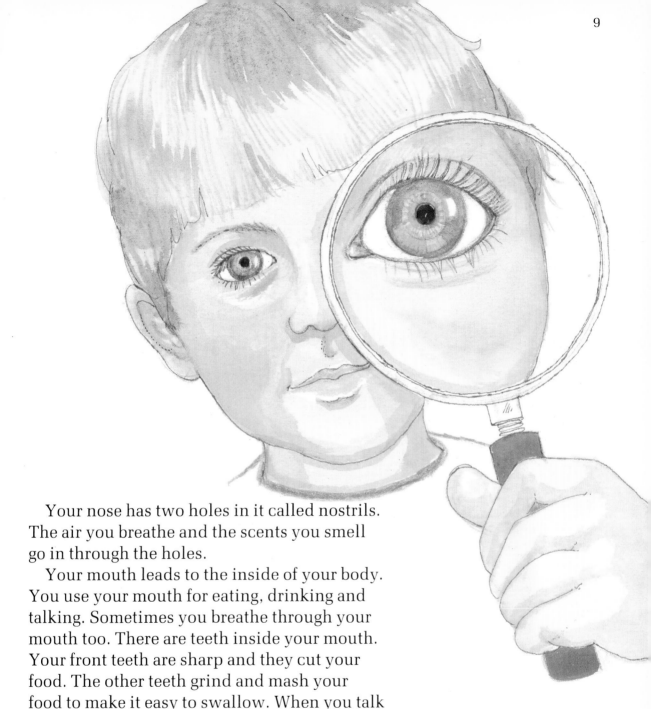

Your nose has two holes in it called nostrils. The air you breathe and the scents you smell go in through the holes.

Your mouth leads to the inside of your body. You use your mouth for eating, drinking and talking. Sometimes you breathe through your mouth too. There are teeth inside your mouth. Your front teeth are sharp and they cut your food. The other teeth grind and mash your food to make it easy to swallow. When you talk your tongue and teeth help you make the right sounds.

Your tongue is always busy. You talk and it helps you to say words. It moves your food when you chew. The little bumps on your tongue help you to taste your food.

Lopsided you

Two eyes, two eyebrows, two ears and two nostrils – your face has two sides, but are they exactly the same?

Look at your face in a mirror. Is one of your eyebrows straighter than the other? And what about your ears – are they in exactly the same place on each side of your head? Now look at

Compare the right and left sides of this girl's face. If you think they are the same, look at the pictures on the next page.

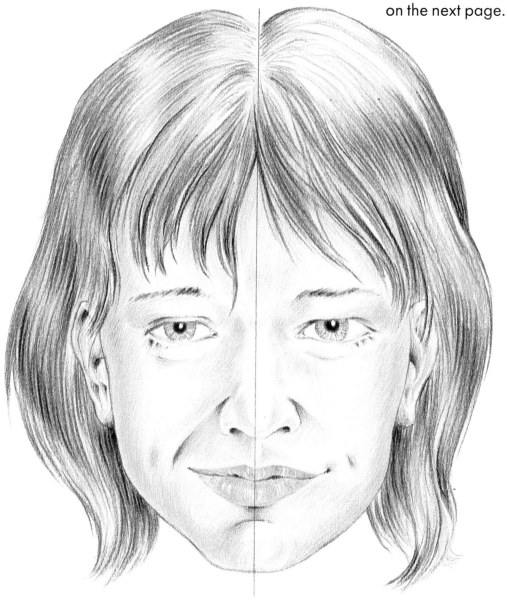

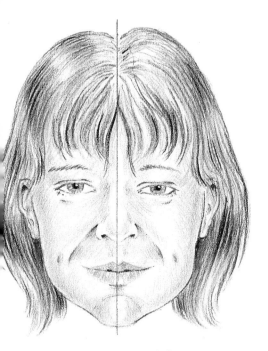

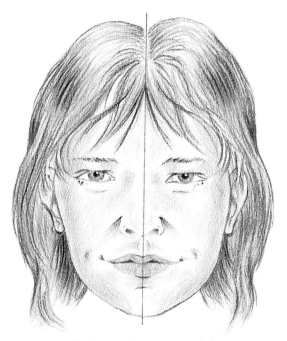

This is the same girl, but the picture is made up only of the **left half** of her face.

And this is the same girl — but this picture is made up of the **right half**!

your mouth. The two sides probably won't match. And no matter how hard you brush your hair, it will never look the same on both sides.

Other parts of you don't match either. Look at your hands. Is one hand bigger than the other? Are your fingers longer or thinner on one hand?

When you get new shoes, is one a bit tighter than the other? There's nothing wrong. Your doctor will tell you it's quite normal.

If you could be divided into two parts, the right-hand side of you wouldn't exactly match the left-hand side. And it's the same for everyone. If you look in a mirror, you will see that the left half of your face is not exactly the same as the right half of your face.

Find a photo of yourself. Hold a mirror along the nose like this. What can you see?

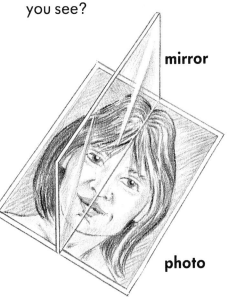

mirror

photo

Your hair

Red, black, brown and blond – hair can be many colours. About 100,000 hairs cover the top of your head. If you pull out a hair, a new one will grow to take its place. Your hair grows and is cut – and grows again. Where does all that hair come from?

Each hair grows out of a tiny hole in your skin. These holes are called hair follicles. At the bottom of each follicle are tiny tubes called veins and arteries. They bring blood to the root of the hair. The hair takes food and oxygen from the blood. This makes the hair grow.

At the opening into the follicle is a little pocket of oil. The oil makes your hair shine.

We like to use our **hair** as a decoration. There are many different styles and fashions to choose from. This girl has bound her hair in braids.

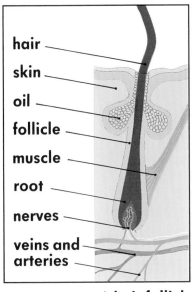

hair

skin

oil

follicle

muscle

root

nerves

veins and
arteries

A **hair follicle**

Each tiny follicle has a muscle too. If you're scared, it feels as if your hair stands on end. It feels this way because tiny muscles move the skin and hair on the top of your head.

Some hair is straight, some is curly. Some hair doesn't grow long. Eyelashes and eyebrows never grow very much. But the hair on the top of your head can grow as much as fifteen centimetres a year.

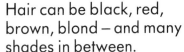

Hair can be black, red, brown, blond — and many shades in between.

Fingernails and toenails

Do you know why you have fingernails and toenails? To protect the ends of your fingers and toes.

Your fingernails and toenails are made of a tough material called keratin. Keratin is formed from hard skin. Animals' claws, hooves and horns are made of the same thing.

Your nails grow from the base, where you see a pale shape that looks like part of the moon. The outer skin at the base of your nails is known as your cuticle.

Your nails grow all the time. If you make a mud pie or play with sand, dirt gets under the tips of your fingernails. So you scrub them and clip them to keep them clean. You clip your toenails straight across so they won't grow back into the flesh at the corners of your toes.

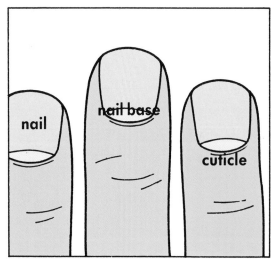

fingernails

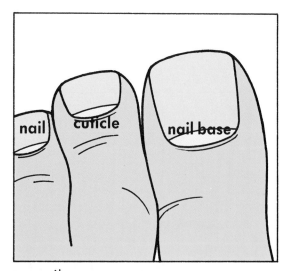

toenails

What is a cell?

All living things – plants, animals and people – are made of cells. You are made of cells.

A cell is the smallest living part of you it is possible to imagine. A cell can be long, short, thin, fat, square or round. It is made of a soft jelly-like material called protoplasm. A cell is so small it can be seen only through a microscope.

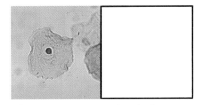

The picture on the left is a magnified photo of a single **cell**. About 6 million skin cells would fit into the empty square on the right.

Working cells

All cells grow and divide. Every minute your body makes more than 3,000 million new cells. Cells make new cells by growing and dividing in two.

In order to live, cells need food and oxygen. Oxygen is in the air. You breathe air. You eat food. Your body changes these a little bit and then your blood is able to carry them to all the cells in your body.

Your cells use up the food and oxygen and give off material cells cannot use. The useless material is called waste products. Your blood carries waste products away from your cells.

Cells do special jobs. A lot of cells joined together is called tissue. Different sorts of tissue joined together make organs, such as your eye or your muscles.

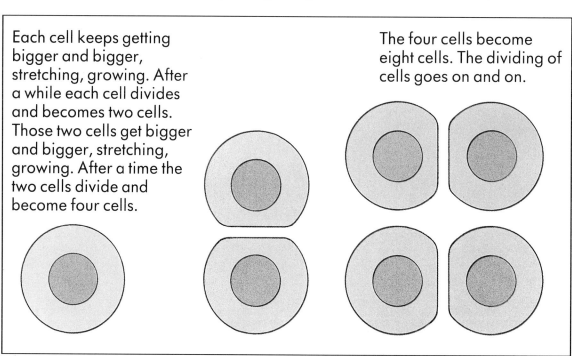

Each cell keeps getting bigger and bigger, stretching, growing. After a while each cell divides and becomes two cells. Those two cells get bigger and bigger, stretching, growing. After a time the two cells divide and become four cells.

The four cells become eight cells. The dividing of cells goes on and on.

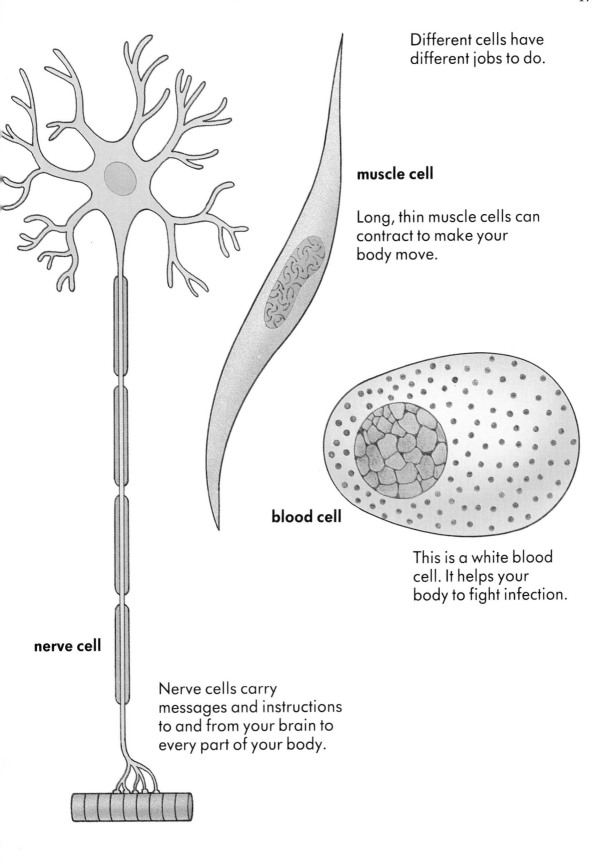

Different cells have different jobs to do.

muscle cell

Long, thin muscle cells can contract to make your body move.

blood cell

This is a white blood cell. It helps your body to fight infection.

nerve cell

Nerve cells carry messages and instructions to and from your brain to every part of your body.

Your skin

Your skin is one of the organs of your body. Some waste products are carried out of your body through your skin when you sweat. And your skin helps keep your body at an even temperature.

All skin is tough, but some parts are tougher than others. The skin on the bottom of your feet is toughest of all. You can scratch and scrape skin, but it will always grow back again.

Some of your skin is quite thick and some is quite thin. Apart from the soles of your feet, the thickest skin is on your back and the thinnest is on your eyelids.

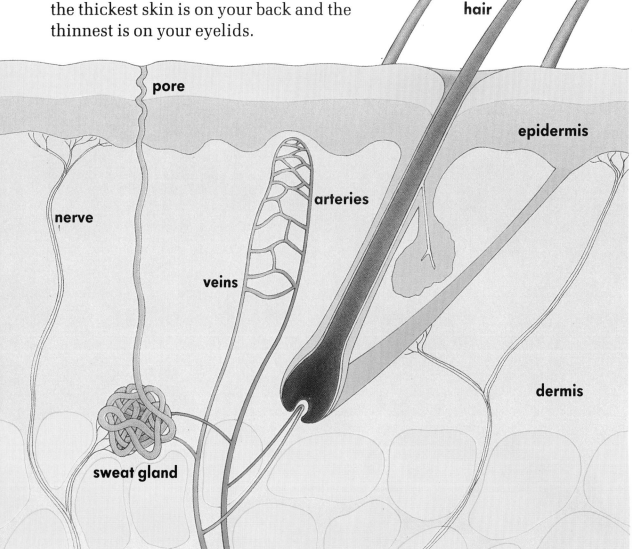

hair

pore

epidermis

arteries

nerve

veins

dermis

sweat gland

When you're cold, goose-pimples, or goose bumps, are raised on your **skin**. These make the hairs stand up and trap more air. The extra layer of air helps keep you warm.

When you're hot you **sweat**. Sweating helps to cool you down.

All skin, even the thinnest, is made up of two layers. The outer layer is called the epidermis and the inner layer is called the dermis.

Skin contains tiny veins and arteries filled with blood, and nerves that help you feel heat, cold and pain. Your skin also contains tiny holes called pores. When you're hot, drops of sweat come out through the pores. As the sweat dries, you feel cooler.

When you're cold, your pores close and no sweat gets out. If you're cold, you shiver. Shivering helps warm you by making your body produce more heat in your muscles.

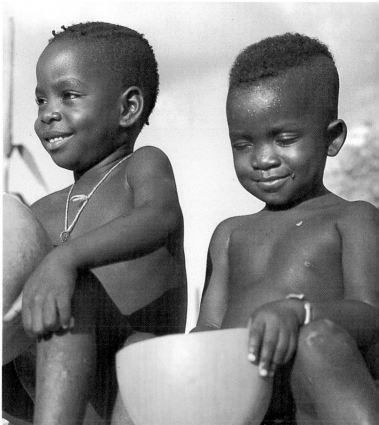

Why do we have skin of a different colour?

People come in many colours. Some have light-brown skins, some dark like the colour of rich chocolate. Skins can be pink, almost white, and some are the colour of gold.

Scientists have spent a long time studying the colours of skin. They have tried to find out why people's skin is a particular colour in different parts of the world. They believe the answer is all to do with the amount of sunshine we enjoy.

Dark-coloured skin contains a large amount of a brown colouring called melanin. Melanin is produced by the body to protect the skin from burning in strong sunshine. This is why many people who come from hot countries have dark skins.

In countries where the sunlight is weaker, dark skin is not important. Here the paler skin colours are best because they allow sunlight to enter the skin, where it helps to make an important substance called vitamin D.

In some cases melanin builds up in small spots called freckles. People who have freckles may get even more if they spend time in the sun.

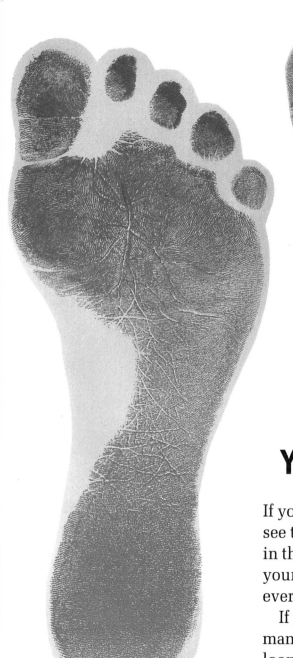
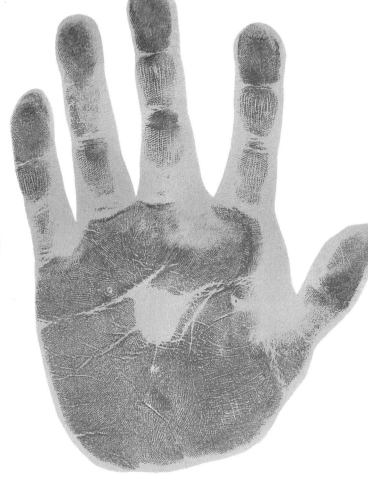

Your very own marks

If you press your finger on a window, you can see the fingerprint you leave there. No one else in the world has fingerprints exactly like yours. And your footprints are different from everyone else's too.

If you look at your fingertips you will see many tiny lines. These lines make patterns of loops and circles. Each finger has a different design. You have ten fingers and ten different fingerprints.

There might be somebody somewhere who looks almost like you. But that person's fingerprints would be different from yours.

23

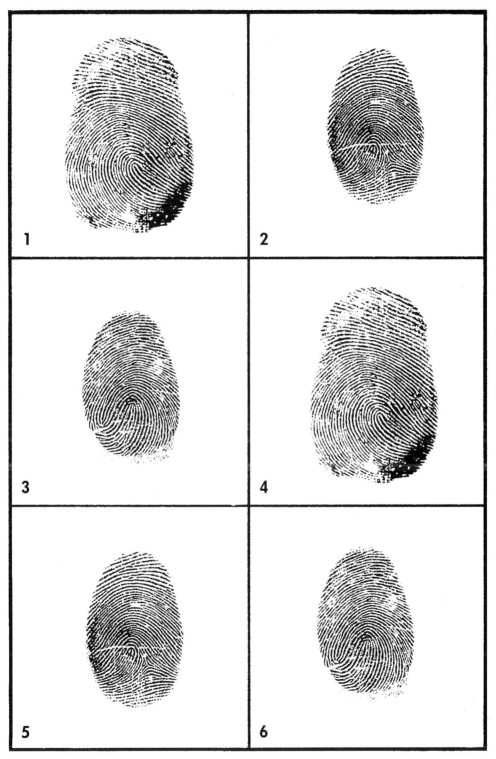

Can you find the matching
pairs of fingerprints?

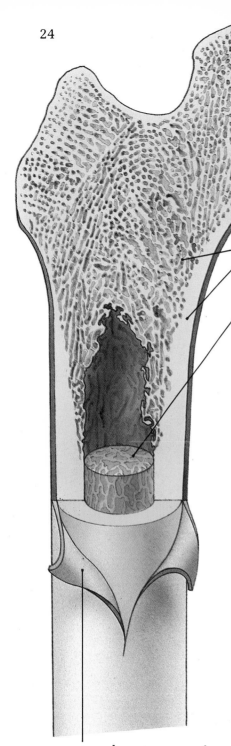

bone

marrow

tough outer covering

This is a **thigh bone**, with the top half cut away to show the different parts.

Bones

You have bones of many shapes and sizes. Leg bones are long. Toe bones are short. Rib bones are rounded. Some bones in your head are flat. The bones in your spine look a little like cotton-reels.

Some bones, like those in the top of your head, can't move. Others, like those in your legs, fit together so that they do move. That's why you bend and move so well.

Your bones are hard. But they are not so hard on the inside as they are on the outside.

Some bones, like those in your legs, are hollow, like tubes. Inside the hollow is bone marrow. Marrow is made up of tissue and fat, tiny veins and arteries, and cells that make new blood cells for your body. Your bones also store important substances called minerals, so that your body can use them when it needs them.

Every day new cells are added to your bones, and they become longer and larger.

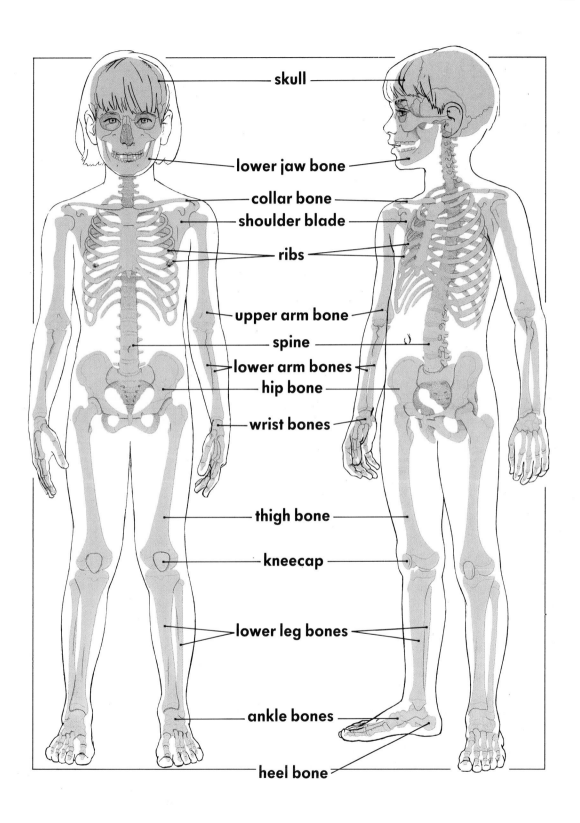

skull

lower jaw bone

collar bone

shoulder blade

ribs

upper arm bone

spine

lower arm bones

hip bone

wrist bones

thigh bone

kneecap

lower leg bones

ankle bones

heel bone

Your body's framework

You have a skeleton inside you. That's what your bones are called when they are all joined together. If you didn't have a skeleton, you'd be floppy like a rag doll. Your skeleton gives shape to your body.

Bones protect your inner organs. The bones in your skull protect your brain. Your ribs protect your heart and lungs.

There is cartilage between most of your bones. Cartilage is softer than bone. It keeps bones from rubbing against each other.

Bones fit together at places called joints. Some joints, like those in your skull, do not move. Other joints, like those in your legs, do move. When you move around, lots of your bones have to work together.

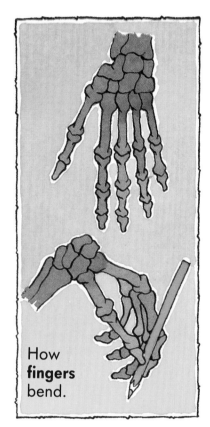

How **fingers** bend.

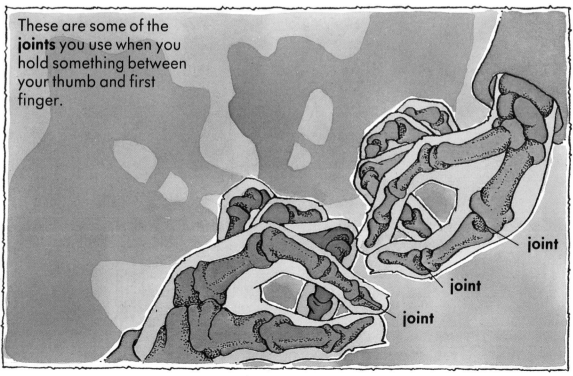

These are some of the **joints** you use when you hold something between your thumb and first finger.

joint

joint

joint

How muscles stretch

Join two lollipop sticks or thin pieces of wood together, using a brass paper fastener.

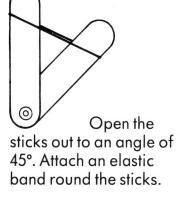

Open the sticks out to an angle of 45°. Attach an elastic band round the sticks.

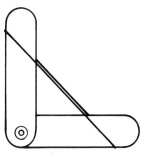

Now pull the sticks open and watch the elastic stretch. Your muscles stretch in the same way.

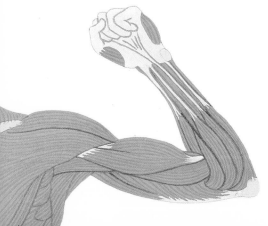

Your muscles

Your body is filled with muscles.

Deep inside you, muscles help your body to work properly. Muscles help food move through your body. And muscles help air move in and out of your lungs.

Some of your muscles are fastened to your bones, and these muscles help you move.

Some muscles that must work hard are joined to your bones by strong, tough cords called tendons. You can feel tendons on the insides of your wrists and at the backs of your ankles. The tendon in your ankle is called the Achilles' tendon. It joins your calf muscles to your heel.

Your leg muscles help you run and skip.

Your arm muscles help you lift and carry things.

Your neck muscles help you hold up your head.

The muscles in your face help you wink and smile and make funny faces.

Your body has more than 600 major muscles. Apart from those that help you move, others help to keep your body working. These are not fastened to your bones.

Muscles in your stomach mix and mash your food. Muscles in your chest help you to breathe. And your heart is a very special kind of extra-strong muscle.

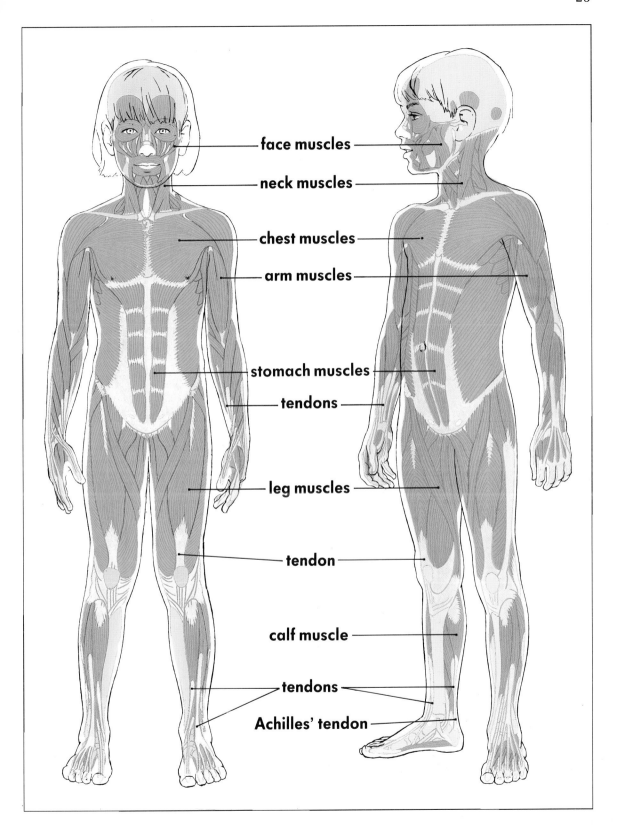

face muscles

neck muscles

chest muscles

arm muscles

stomach muscles

tendons

leg muscles

tendon

calf muscle

tendons

Achilles' tendon

The way you move

Run, jump, bend, stretch. You can do all these things because you have muscles. You can move because you have muscles. Muscles that help you move are fastened to your bones and are elastic, like rubber bands. They can stretch out and draw back together again.

Some muscles, like the big ones in your arms and legs, have strong cords called tendons at the ends. The muscles are fastened to your bones by these tendons.

Muscles work together in groups. As some of them tighten and become shorter, the other muscles in the group get longer. That's what happens when you bend your elbow or knee and straighten it again. If you didn't have muscles, you wouldn't be able to move or even stand.

Think how many **muscles** these children must be using. Try lifting a ball like this and feel how many muscles are working.

Breathe in!

Take a deep breath. Listen to the air being sucked into your body.

When you breathe, air enters your nose. The inside of your nose warms the air. Little hairs in your nose catch the dust in the air. The wetness in your nose catches most of the germs you breathe in.

The warm, clean air goes down a tube called the trachea and into your lungs.

Your lungs are in your chest and you have two of them. Your ribs make a kind of cage around your lungs that protects them.

Below your lungs is a strong muscle called the diaphragm. Your diaphragm and the muscles fastened to your ribs move your chest in and out, in and out. When your chest moves out, fresh air comes into your lungs. When your chest moves in, used air leaves your lungs.

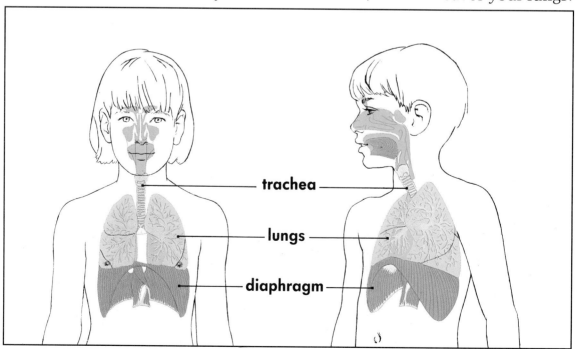

trachea

lungs

diaphragm

When the musician plays the concertina, he pulls it open to fill it with air and then squeezes the air out again. Your rib cage and diaphragm work the same way – pulling air into your **lungs** and squeezing it out again.

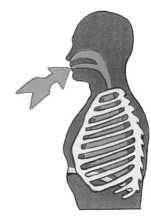

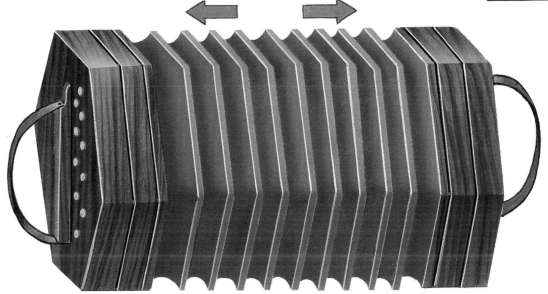

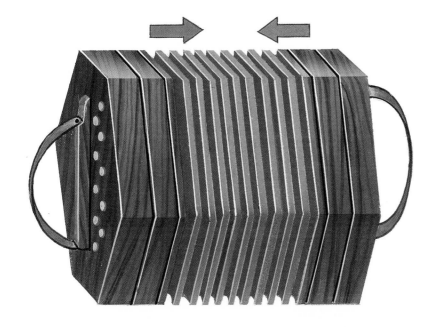

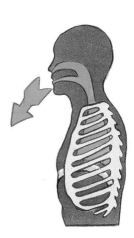

The blood pump

Bump, bump, bump. If you put your hand on your chest, you can feel something beating. It's your heart.

Your heart is a muscle about the size of your fist. It acts like a pump. Its job is to pump blood around your body.

The left-hand side of your heart pumps blood through tubes called arteries. The blood is fresh. It carries oxygen from your lungs to all the cells of your body.

Blood flows back to your heart through different tubes called veins. This blood is not fresh. It has given up its oxygen. Now it carries carbon dioxide from all the cells in your body.

The right-hand side of your heart pumps the used blood through your lungs. There the blood swaps the carbon dioxide for oxygen. Then your heart pumps the fresh blood into your arteries and back through your body.

Blood moves fast. Blood leaving your heart right now will travel all the way to your toes and back again in about one minute.

If doctors want to know how fast your heart is beating, they take your pulse. They can feel how fast the blood is being pushed through the artery in your wrist.

Your **heart** is about the same size as your fist.

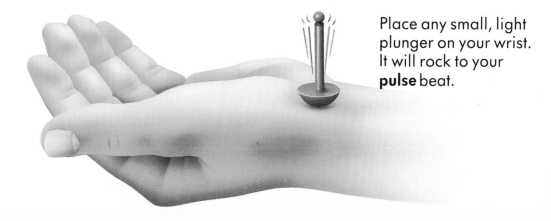

Place any small, light plunger on your wrist. It will rock to your **pulse** beat.

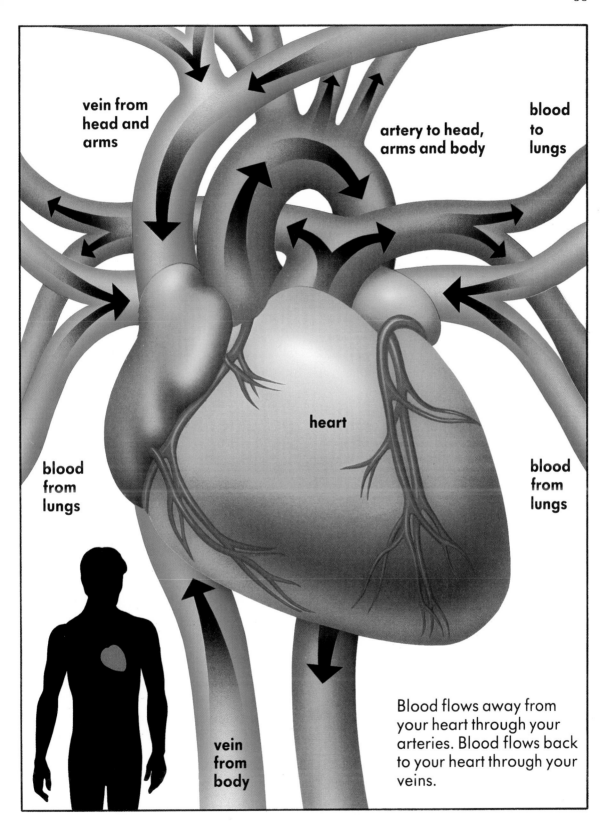

vein from head and arms

artery to head, arms and body

blood to lungs

blood from lungs

heart

blood from lungs

vein from body

Blood flows away from your heart through your arteries. Blood flows back to your heart through your veins.

Your blood

Your blood carries oxygen to your cells. Every cell in your body needs oxygen in order to live. Bone cells, muscle cells, brain cells – all must have oxygen.

Every cell in your body gives off waste materials which your body cannot use. Bone cells, muscle cells, brain cells – all give off waste materials. This is why you have thousands of arteries and veins to take the blood all round your body.

Your blood carries waste materials away from your cells. The waste materials must be cleaned out of your blood. That happens as the blood passes through your kidneys. Your kidneys are behind your stomach near your spine.

Your body has between two and four litres of blood. If you cut yourself and lose some, your body makes new blood to take its place.

Blood cells are made in the marrow inside your bones. New cells are made every second. Your marrow bone makes more than 100 million new blood cells every minute.

Blood has red cells in it. The red cells are workers. They carry oxygen and carbon dioxide. Blood has white cells in it too. These are fighters. They kill germs and help you to stay strong and healthy.

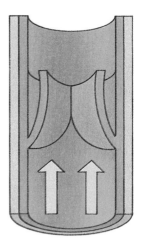

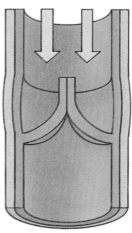

Valves in your blood vessels make sure that blood moves only in one direction – for example, up the veins in your legs. As each heartbeat pushes blood along, the flaps in the valves open and let blood through. In the pause before the next heartbeat, the valve shuts, stopping the blood from flowing backwards.

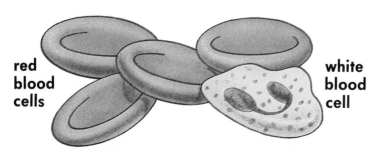

red blood cells   **white blood cell**

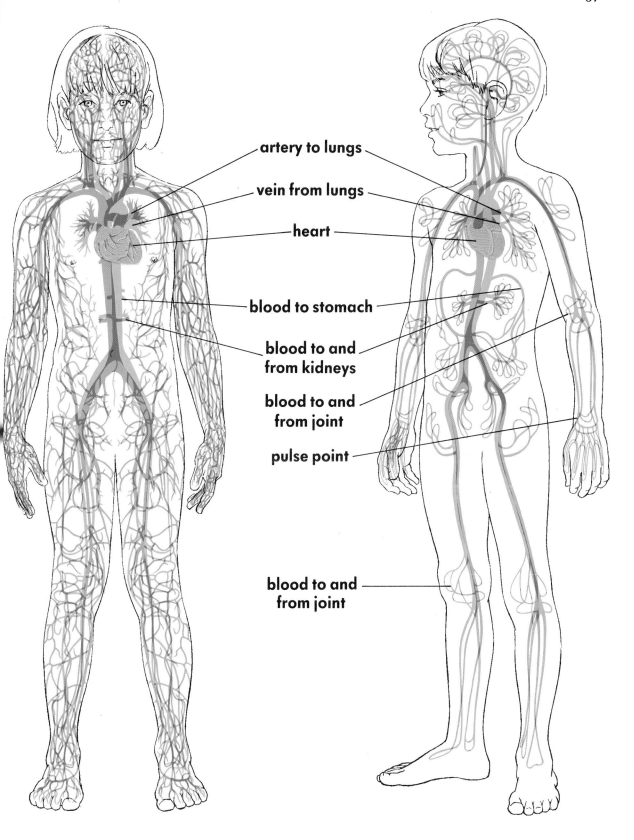

artery to lungs

vein from lungs

heart

blood to stomach

blood to and
from kidneys

blood to and
from joint

pulse point

blood to and
from joint

Your body can mend itself

Your body has its own way of mending itself. It heals itself. When you hurt yourself, your cells begin to do special jobs.

Let's pretend you've cut your hand on a piece of glass. The cut bleeds. Almost at once the blood coming from the cut begins to get thick. The cells stick together and cover the cut. Then the blood becomes hard. It makes a kind of cap called a scab, over the cut.

Under the scab other cells are working.

Germs may have got into the cut. White cells in your blood eat up the germs.

As soon as you cut yourself, the **cells** of your body set to work to mend the wound.

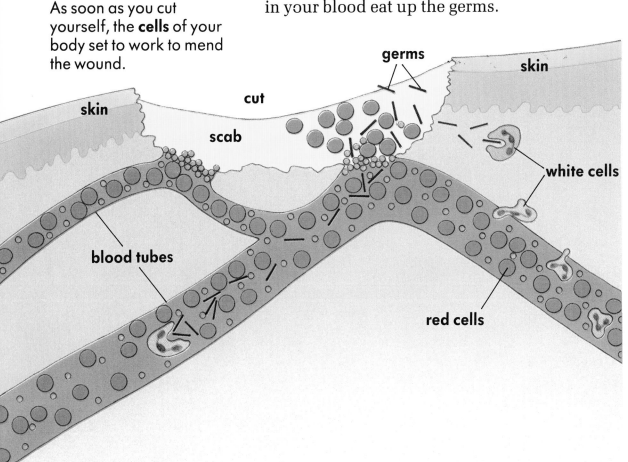

germs

skin

cut

skin

scab

white cells

blood tubes

red cells

Under the **scab** on this boy's grazed knee, new skin is growing.

The skin cells along the edges of the wound grow and divide, grow and divide. New cells take the place of some of those that were hurt by the glass.

Other cells do another job. These are special healing cells. They make a kind of net that joins the edges of the cut together. Each day this net gets thicker, tougher and stronger. It is called a scab.

After a while the scab falls off. Then you can see a scar.

Healthy healing

1 Jimmy's fallen over. He's cut his knee on a sharp stone. Look what's happening under his skin.

2 Look out! Here come the germs to invade Jimmy's cut. The white blood cells line up to defend Jimmy.

3 The white blood cells set off. "It's our job to gobble up the germs. Here we go!"

4

"Come on, cells. Line up. We have to stick together."
Jimmy's cells bunch together and mend his cut.

5

"Squeeze together, everyone. It's our job to make a cover for the cut.

It's called a scab, and it stops more germs getting in."

6

ONE WEEK LATER

And, between them, Jimmy's cells have done a very good job.

Things that go bump

"Ouch!"

Sometimes you bump your ankle, or your leg or your elbow. The bump pushes a muscle against a bone, and tiny veins and arteries break. You have a bruise.

A bruise is a sort of upside-down cut. When you cut yourself, blood comes out of the cut. But blood does not come out of a bruise. Instead, it leaks underneath the top layer of your skin. The blood shows through your skin as dark blue or black.

As the bruise heals it may change colour. Sometimes it changes to purple, then to lavender, then to yellow. Each colour is lighter than the last. This means that the blood is moving back into your body. The bruised muscle is getting well.

Have you ever burned your hand? The burnt spot puffs up and you get a blister. A blister is a kind of puffy little pocket in the layers of your skin. The top layer of skin pulls away from the layers under it, and the space fills with liquid. The top layer keeps germs from getting into the blister. Then your cells start to do their healing job just as they do when you have a cut. Slowly the liquid moves back into your body and your blister heals.

When you fall over and **bruise** your knees, you bleed a little underneath your skin. Even though you can't see the blood, it still hurts!

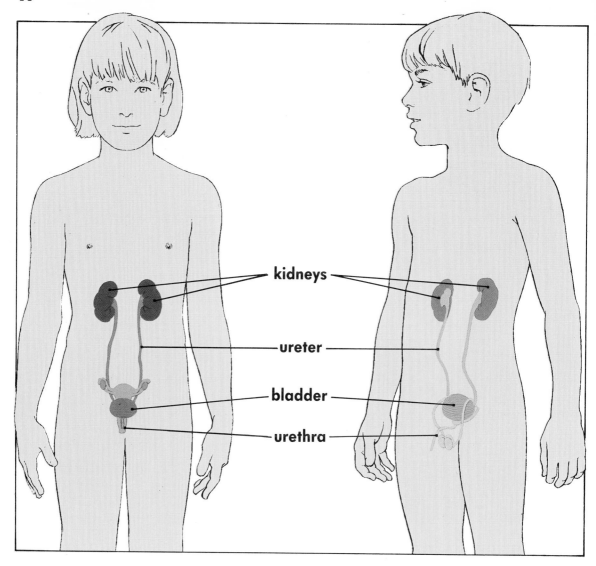

kidneys

ureter

bladder

urethra

The work of your kidneys

In your back, on each side of your spine and just under your ribs, are your kidneys. They are about half the size of your heart and they are shaped like beans.

Kidneys do an important job for your body – they help keep your blood clean.

Your blood takes waste products – things your body cannot use – away from your cells. Your blood passes through your kidneys and your kidneys take the waste products out of your blood.

The kidneys then need to get rid of this waste. They do this by making a liquid called urine which contains the waste. Urine leaves your kidneys through two tubes called ureters. The ureters take the urine to your bladder.

Your bladder is a stretchy bag made of thin sheets of muscle. When it is full, you feel as if you need to go to the toilet. When you do, the bladder squeezes the urine out through a tube called the urethra.

Your kidneys make droplets of **urine** which carry away the waste material from your blood.

kidney

ureter

Every day, 170 litres of blood pass through your **kidneys.**

Flight or fight

Imagine you are outside your friend's home, playing ball. Wham! The ball bounces too high – right through a neighbour's window. Suddenly a large head appears from behind the bushes. An angry voice booms, "Whose ball is this?" Your heart thumps, you breathe quickly and you go pale. You want to run away.

Has something like this ever happened to you? It's the body's natural way of protecting itself. This is what is happening. Messages are sent speeding to two special places just above your kidneys. These parts of your body make a chemical called adrenalin, which rushes into your blood. Then your heart beats faster, so the adrenalin is pumped around your body.

Now you are ready for an emergency – your stomach stops working and your muscles are all set for action. The aim is to get you out of danger. The feeling that adrenalin causes is often called 'flight or fight', because you suddenly need to run away or stand and face the danger.

Adrenalin is a hormone. Hormones are powerful messengers which are made in places called glands, like those above your kidneys. You have other glands in your body which make different kinds of hormones, each with a different job to do.

One gland, which is in your brain, is often called the master gland. This gland controls your growth.

In your neck you have a gland which makes a hormone to control how quickly oxygen and food are used up in your body. Two other glands in the same place control the mineral called calcium you have in your blood.

Another gland near your stomach makes a hormone which controls the amount of sugar in your body.

Body facts

The heart pumps about 6,500 litres of blood each day.

If a man's legs could move as quickly as an ant's legs, he would run at more than 160 km per hour.

The human sense of smell is very weak. But the male emperor moth has a strong sense of smell. It can detect a female at a distance of 11 km.

ONE...

There are about 100,000 hairs on a person's head.

If you could spread a pair of lungs out flat, they would cover an area as big as a tennis court.

The giant squid has the largest eyeball in the animal kingdom – it is 38 cm in diameter. The human eyeball is only about 25 mm across.

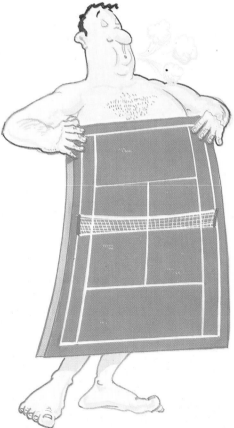

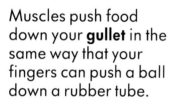

Muscles push food down your **gullet** in the same way that your fingers can push a ball down a rubber tube.

What happens when you eat?

Crunch, crunch, crunch! You are just beginning your favourite meal – but have you ever wondered exactly where your food goes when you eat? And what happens to it when it's inside your body?

First of all, when your food gets inside your mouth, it has to be broken up into smaller parts so that it is easy to swallow. This is the job of your teeth, which grind and mix your food. Inside your mouth there are groups of cells called glands. These glands make a liquid called saliva, which is mixed with your food to help it slip down. Your tongue mixes the food with saliva and then pushes it to the back of your mouth.

Once your food has been swallowed it starts on its way through your body. It passes from your mouth down a tube called the gullet. By the time you have counted to eight the food will have entered your stomach. Now it is on its way to be changed, so that your body can use it.

Your stomach goes on with the job your teeth began. It squeezes and mixes and mashes and adds more juices to the food. By the time the food is ready to leave your stomach, it is just like a kind of toothpaste.

Food comes down the **gullet**.

It enters the **stomach**.

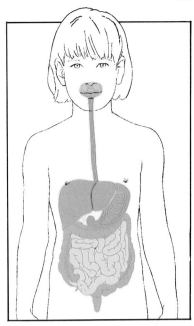

Next, it goes through the **small intestine**.

And finally through the **large intestine**.

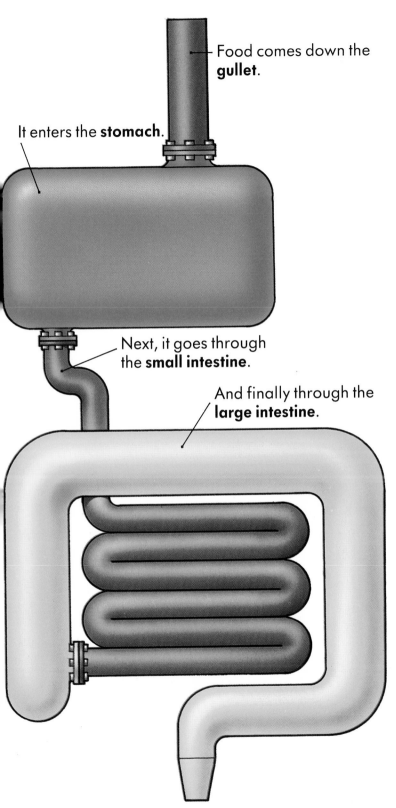

When you eat, your food has to go through many metres of tube. The picture above shows how the tube fits inside you.

The tube inside you is working all the time, just like a well-oiled machine. This picture shows you how it is made up of different parts.

The 6 metre food processor

After your food has been in your stomach for about two to five hours, it moves down into your small intestine. Here, powerful chemicals called enzymes and a juice called bile soak into the food and start to change it. The enzymes are very thorough. Any scrap of food which escapes one attack runs into another further down the small intestine. The food may stay in your small intestine for up to forty hours. Soon the food is no longer hamburger, beans or apple. It has been broken down, or digested, into very tiny pieces called molecules. These molecules are so small they can pass through the walls of the small intestine and into the blood. The blood carries the molecules into the cells where they will help you grow and stay fit.

Food that your body can't use passes from the small intestine into another long tube called the large intestine. At the end of this is the rectum where waste food leaves the body.

Do you know how many metres of **small** and **large intestine** are coiled inside your body? Take a ball of string and carefully measure the drawing to find out.

Enzymes and **digestive juices** are waiting in your small intestine to break up your food. All the good things you need can then be used by your body.

Entrance to the intestine.

Enzymes rule

Bile is best

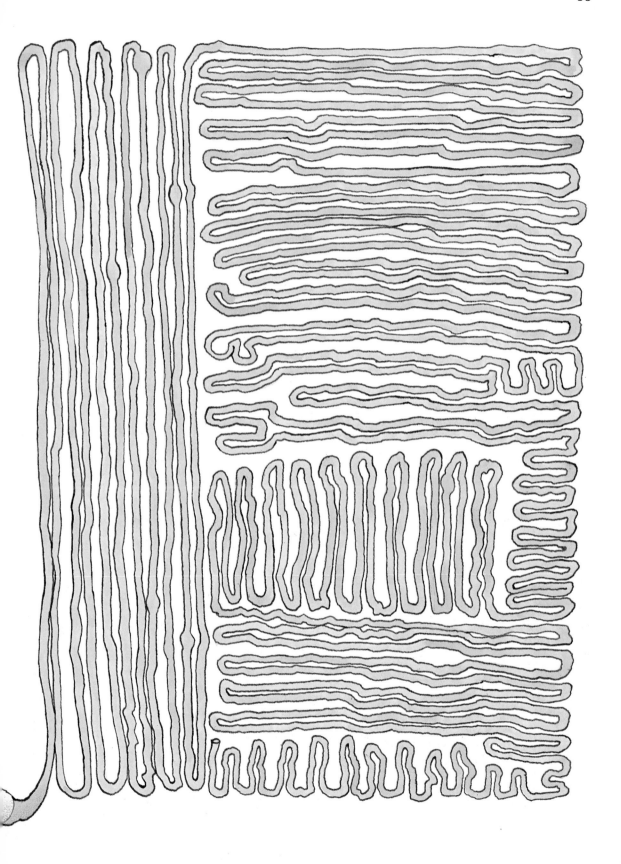

Food is fuel

Your body is a machine. It is like a car but instead of petrol it needs food to keep it going. Some foods make it work much better than others.

Some foods keep you **healthy**.

Food gives you energy. It helps you to grow and to keep healthy. Food is made up of different parts called proteins, fats and carbohydrates.

Proteins help your body to grow. They help your body to make muscles, skin and other organs, and blood. They also help your body to mend when it is damaged.

Some foods help your body **grow**.

Some foods help your body stay **warm**.

Carbohydrates and fats give you energy. They help your body stay warm.

Food also contains vitamins and minerals, water and tough parts like potato skins which we call roughage.

There are many different minerals such as calcium and iron, and vitamins such as A, B, C and D. They keep your body healthy. Water is important because it helps make up your blood and carry the food you need around your body. You need roughage to help your muscles push your food through your stomach.

You can't just eat **protein** — you need something more.

Fruit is good for you too — but not by itself.

Carbohydrates on their own will tip the balance too!

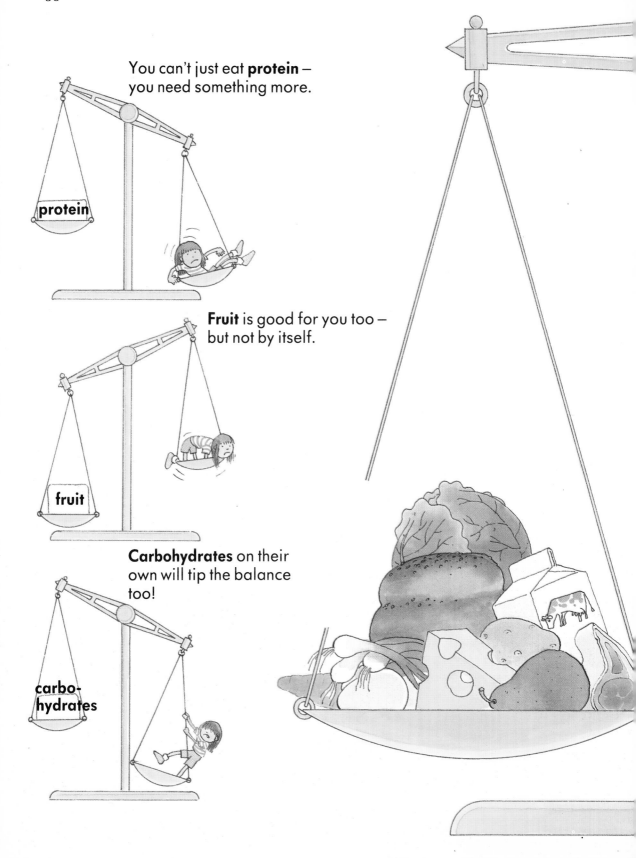

A balanced diet

Imagine a pair of scales that are special scales to show the balance of the foods you eat. Perhaps your favourite foods are meat, eggs, milk and cheese. Let's put all these on to the scales. Just watch them tip the balance! These foods are all good for you – but they're all proteins. The scales are showing you that you need a varied diet with average-sized portions of lots of different foods to keep you healthy.

You know you need carbohydrates and fats to give you energy. So you should eat potatoes, bread, rice or cereals. Don't worry too much about the fats – you get them in almost every food you eat without trying. Protein for growth is found in meat, fish, eggs, milk and cheese. So you should try to eat a little of one of these at every meal. You should also try to eat plenty of fresh fruit and vegetables to give you the vitamins and minerals you need.

58

Good food chart

	protein	fat	carbo-hydrate	vitamins	minerals	fibre
wholemeal bread				B	iron calcium	
wholemeal pasta				B	iron calcium	
brown rice				B	iron calcium	
cheese				A D	iron calcium	none
butter, margarine			none	A D	calcium	none
eggs				A B C	iron calcium	none
milk				A B D	calcium	none
yoghurt				A D	calcium	none
fresh fish				A B D	iron calcium	none
tinned fish				A B D	iron calcium	none
red meat				B	iron calcium	

	high			medium		low
	protein	fat	carbo-hydrate	vitamins	minerals	fibre
chicken, turkey				A B	iron calcium	
liver, kidney				A B D	iron calcium	
lettuce		none		A C	iron calcium	
vegetables with green leaves		none		A C	calcium	
root vegetables		none		A C	iron calcium	
apples, pears				A C	iron calcium	
oranges, grapefruit				A C	iron calcium	
tomatoes				A C	iron calcium	
fresh peas				A B C	iron calcium	
dried beans				A B	iron calcium	
nuts				B	iron calcium	

Menu One

You will need:

2 tomatoes
1 small onion
1 small can tuna fish
pepper
oil
1 teacup brown rice
1 ½ teacups of chicken
   stock
a sharp knife
a tin opener
a saucepan
a fork
a plate

Brown rice risotto

This risotto uses tuna fish and tomatoes, but almost any savoury food can be chopped up and added instead. Try mushrooms, ham or peas. This is enough for three people.

Chop up the tomatoes and onion.
Open the tuna fish, drain it and flake it up on a plate with a fork. Season with a little pepper.
Heat the oil in the saucepan.
Cook the chopped onion and rice for five minutes. Now add the stock, put the lid on the pan and cook for thirty minutes on a low heat.

Add the chopped tomatoes and tuna. Cook for another ten minutes – and eat while it's warm.

Risotto is good served with a mixed green salad of lettuce, sliced cucumber and chopped green pepper.

Fresh fruit salad

Like the risotto, almost
anything goes!
Try an apple, an orange,
a grapefruit, a few
grapes, all chopped up
into mouth-sized bites.
Other fruits to try are
peaches, strawberries,
cherries and pears.

Sprinkle lemon juice over
the chopped fruit to stop it
going brown. If you must
make it sweeter, pour a
little pure orange juice
over the salad.
On hot days, this is
delicious if it's been left at
the bottom of the
refrigerator for an hour.

Menu Two

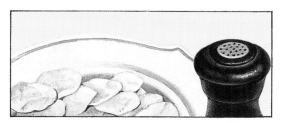

Potato bake

This is enough for three people.

You will need:

450 gm potatoes
1 onion
100 gm Cheddar cheese
25 gm margarine
pepper
a potato peeler
a knife
a chopping board
a colander
a plate   a grater
a 600 ml ovenproof dish

Turn the oven on to gas
mark 4, 180°C.
Peel the potatoes and
slice them thinly.
Rinse them under cold
running water in the
colander. Peel the onion
and chop it up.

Grate the cheese on to the
plate. Now mix the onion
and cheese together.
Rub some of the
margarine around the
inside of the ovenproof
dish.
Put half the slices of
potato on to the bottom of
the ovenproof dish.
Sprinkle on some pepper.
Spread the onion and
cheese mixture over the
potatoes in the dish.
Cover with the second half
of the potatoes and
sprinkle on some more
pepper. Now dab the rest
of the margarine on top.
Bake until the potatoes
are golden brown. This
takes about an hour.
Serve with a green
vegetable such as
cabbage or broccoli.

Fruity apple bake

If you time it right, this tasty pudding will be ready for you to eat when you've finished your potato bake.

You will need:

1 cooking apple for each person
1 tablespoon raisins or sultanas for each person
margarine
water
baking foil
a sharp knife
an apple corer

Turn the oven on to Gas Mark 6, 200°C.
To stop the apple bursting in the oven, slit the skin about half-way up.
Carefully take out the core of the apple with the apple corer.
Lay the apple on a piece of baking foil and put the raisins into the middle.
Add a knob of margarine to the raisins.

Now put a tablespoon of water around the bottom of the apple. Gather up the foil into a neat parcel and bake for forty-five minutes.

All these foods might be nice as a snack, but they don't make a balanced meal.

Junk food

Junk foods are foods such as crisps, jam and ice cream. Some aren't bad for you, but they aren't very good for you either. Some of them contain a lot of sugar, others have a lot of fat – far more than your body needs – and not much else. It wouldn't hurt your body if you never had any of them. But some of them are fun and a little of them sometimes won't hurt you.

Many junk foods have hardly any roughage in them. Roughage is the tough part of fruits and vegetables which your body cannot digest. Without roughage, there would be hardly anything for the muscles in your intestine to push, and they would stop working properly.

You would soon be very unhealthy if you only ate things like ice cream and potato crisps. You wouldn't get enough of the things that your body needs, such as protein, vitamins and roughage. And you would have too much of the things that you only need a little of, such as sugar and fat.

Ice cream has some vitamins and minerals in it, but it also has a lot of sugar.

Brainy business

Think of a huge walnut. Some people say that's what your brain looks like! Your brain fills most of the space in your head, starting from behind your eyebrows. Put your hands to your head and feel the hard bone, called your skull. Like the shell of a walnut, this bone protects the soft brain inside.

Your brain is quite large and heavy. By the time a person is six years old, the brain has reached its full weight of about 1.4 kilograms. It is full of millions of tiny cells which let you think, feel, remember and control your body's movements. The cells in your brain never rest. They are at work all the time, even when you are asleep.

Brain cells are different from the other cells in your body, which can mend themselves if they are hurt. Brain cells can't do this – and once they have worn out they can't be replaced either. You had most of your brain cells when you were born. When you get very old you may find it hard to remember things. This is natural, and one of the reasons is because you have lost many of the brain cells you once had. Your brain cells need food and oxygen to keep them going. Food and oxygen are found in your blood, and your heart pumps blood to your brain all the time. It travels there in tiny blood tubes called capillaries. There are many of these tiny tubes all over your brain.

Messages travel to and from your **brain** along pathways called **nerves**. They branch into smaller and smaller nerves that reach every part of your body.

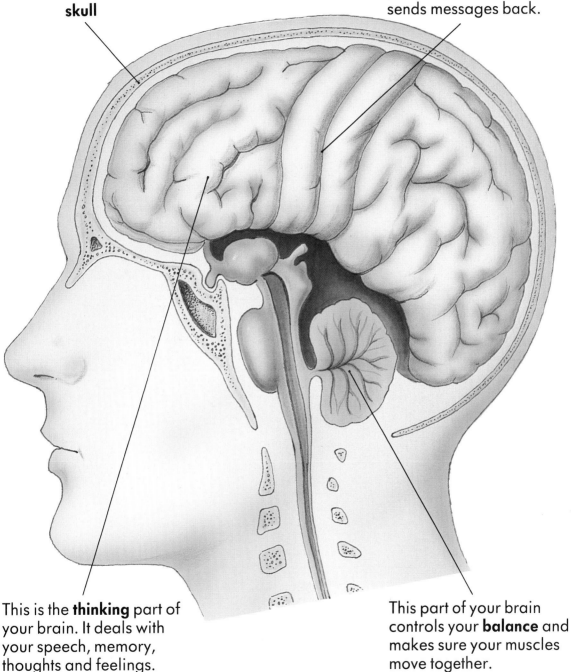

Your brain is made up of different parts. Each one has its own job to do.

skull

The **message centre** is the part of your brain which takes messages from all parts of your body and sends messages back.

This is the **thinking** part of your brain. It deals with your speech, memory, thoughts and feelings.

This part of your brain controls your **balance** and makes sure your muscles move together.

The memory store

Your brain is made up of different parts. In the thinking part of your brain – sometimes called your mind – you deal with all the many different activities that help you make sense of your life. Thoughts, feelings, decisions and ideas all go on here.

Your brain is your memory or knowledge store. All the things you have ever learned are stored to be remembered when you need them. Even things you think you've forgotten can suddenly come back to you years later.

Facts you have learned at school, like 2 x 2 or how to spell cat are stored here. But facts are only some of the things put away in your brain to be used again. Many things that have happened to you are stored away too – like going to a friend's party, being stung by a wasp, playing on the beach. You may think you've forgotten all about them, then years later they come into your mind as clear as when they first happened. You can also remember your feelings about things – not just that the wasp stung you, but how you felt at the time.

All the things that have happened to you become very important for your future. They help you to make decisions. When you need to make a choice about something, all the experiences you've had in the past and all the feelings and thoughts you have now, come together and help you to decide. Because of your memory, your mind is different from any-one else's.

Memory test

Here's a game to test your memory.
You need at least two people to play.

You will need:

paper and pencils
a watch with a second
    hand
a tray
fifteen objects

Choose one person to be the tester. Ask the players to go out of the room. The tester stays behind and lays out about fifteen objects on a tray. Small everyday things, like a pencil, a rubber, a cup and a coin are a good idea, but you could also add some more unusual

objects, like a feather or a piece of cheese.
When all the objects are on the tray, the tester calls back the players.
Now the tester lets them look at the objects for ten seconds. Then he or she quickly puts the tray out of sight.
To test their memories, the players now write down the objects they can remember.
Did anyone remember everything? Was it easier to remember the everyday objects or the more unusual ones?

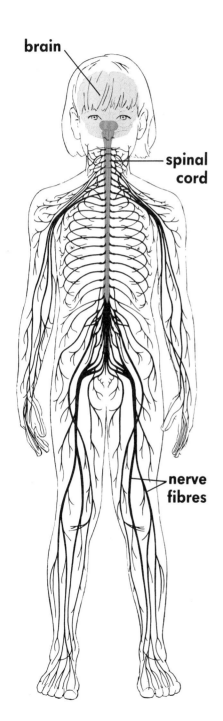

brain

spinal cord

nerve fibres

The control centre

"Ouch!" You've bumped your elbow. It hurts. But you only know this because your brain tells you so. Here's how.

Your brain is the control centre of your body. It receives messages from all parts of your body – and sends back messages in reply. Messages between your brain and the other parts of your body move fast. They can zip up from your feet and back again more than thirty times in one second!

The messages are sent along tiny cords or fibres called nerves. There are thousands of nerves inside your body. They are like tiny telephone wires which your body uses to talk to your brain. Most of these nerves link up to your spinal cord and travel along it to your brain. Your spinal cord is in your spine, which runs down the centre of your back.

Nerves don't just let you know when you've hurt yourself. They carry messages about heat and cold to your brain too. They also carry messages between your brain and your heart, lungs, stomach, intestines and other organs. Your brain keeps these organs working all the time – you couldn't stop your heart or lungs even if you tried. Nerves from your eyes, ears, mouth and nose also carry messages to your brain. Then your brain tells you about the message.

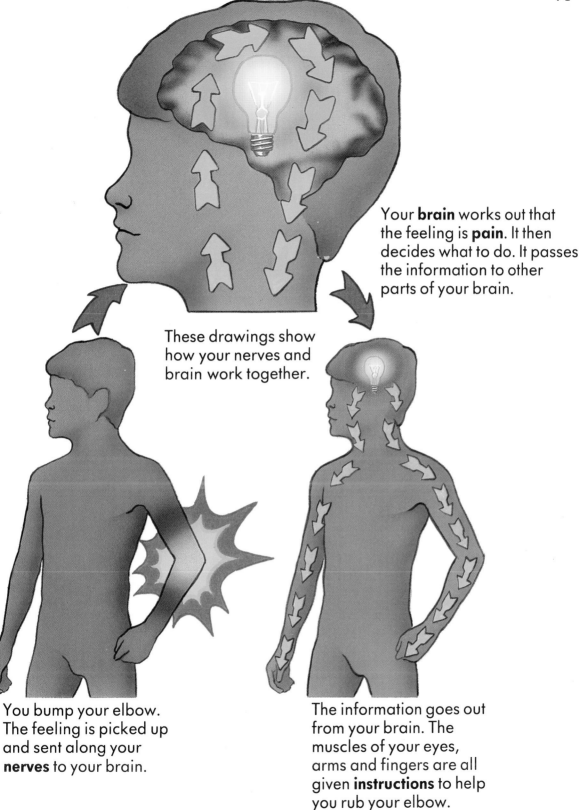

Your **brain** works out that the feeling is **pain**. It then decides what to do. It passes the information to other parts of your brain.

These drawings show how your nerves and brain work together.

You bump your elbow. The feeling is picked up and sent along your **nerves** to your brain.

The information goes out from your brain. The muscles of your eyes, arms and fingers are all given **instructions** to help you rub your elbow.

The blink of an eye

Have you ever tried not to blink when someone moves a hand towards your eye? When you touch something hot or sharp, you jerk your finger away quickly. These are what we call reflex actions. Most reflex actions are actions which we do not control. We do not have to think about them. We have not learned them, we are born with them. Reflex actions are very important, they help to keep us alive.

Sometimes we can control our reflex actions. Think of having an injection. When you know the doctor or nurse is going to stick the needle into your arm, you let your brain take control. If you didn't, you would jerk away, just like you would from any other sharp prick.

A famous Russian scientist called Pavlov made a study of reflex actions. Pavlov noticed that when dogs see their bowls of food, their mouths get wet with saliva. This is a reflex that they have been born with. Pavlov then tried ringing a bell every time the dogs were given some food. Soon the dogs made saliva every time they heard the bell, even if there was no food. They had learned that the bell and the food went together, and so their mouths watered. He proved that the dogs had reflex actions which they had learned. We call this kind of reflex a learned, or conditioned, reflex.

This dog's mouth makes saliva as soon as he sees a tin. He has **learned** that his food comes out of a tin.

This experiment will help you learn about reflexes. You need a friend. Sit in a chair with one leg crossed over the other. The top leg should hang loose.
Now ask your friend to tap you just under your kneecap, with the side of his hand – not too hard! Your leg should suddenly shoot out. But you didn't have to think about it, did you?
This is an example of a reflex action.

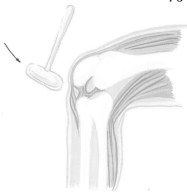

The **reflex point** is just below the kneecap.

Speak for yourself

Take a deep breath. Now let the air out slowly, saying "Ahhh!" You'll only be able to make this sound while there's air in your lungs. When you run out of air there'll be no sound. This proves how important your lungs are for talking.

Now tip your head back and put your fingers at the bottom of your neck, on your throat.

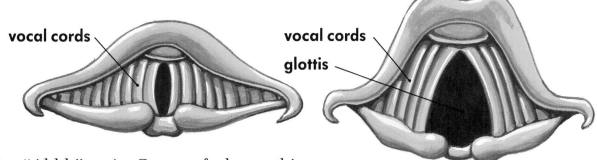

vocal cords

vocal cords
glottis

Say "Ahhh" again. Can you feel something moving? This is your voice-box or larynx.

Your larynx is like a box with two pieces of skin stretched across it. These are your vocal cords. The opening between them is called your glottis. When you talk or sing, air from your lungs is pushed through your glottis. This makes your vocal cords shake, or vibrate. And when they vibrate they make a sound. You can see how this works if you blow up a balloon and pinch the neck. Nothing happens. But as soon as you stretch the neck of the balloon to make a narrow slit, the air escapes and you hear a squealing sound. Your larynx works a bit like the slit in the balloon.

As soon as you were born, you could make sounds. Air from your lungs moved your vocal cords – and you cried. People understood what these sounds meant, but you hadn't learned to talk.

As you grew you found that you could use your tongue, teeth and lips to help you make different sounds. By using special muscles to change the size and shape of the spaces inside your mouth and throat, you could make all kinds of sounds. You said things like "muh", "duh" and "eee". Then you began to copy the sounds of people around you. You made sounds that had a meaning, like "mama", "dada" and "me".

When you talk, air from your lungs is pushed through the opening between your **vocal cords**.

Your **larynx** works a bit like the slit in the balloon. Air escapes through the slit and you hear a sound.

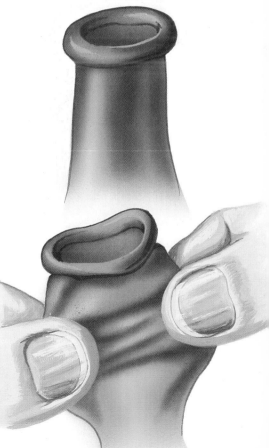

Use your voice

No one else's voice is exactly like yours. And your voice isn't always exactly the same. But people usually know you by your voice.

You use your lips, tongue and teeth when you speak. You also use the soft part in the roof of your mouth and the muscles in your jaws, nose and throat. These parts of you are different in some way from those of any other person. And the way you use these parts is different from the way another person uses their voice parts.

These are pictures of two different **voices** saying the word 'baby'. They were made on a voice print machine. Although the word is the same, the voices made quite different pictures.

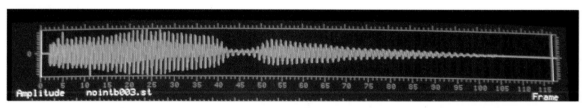

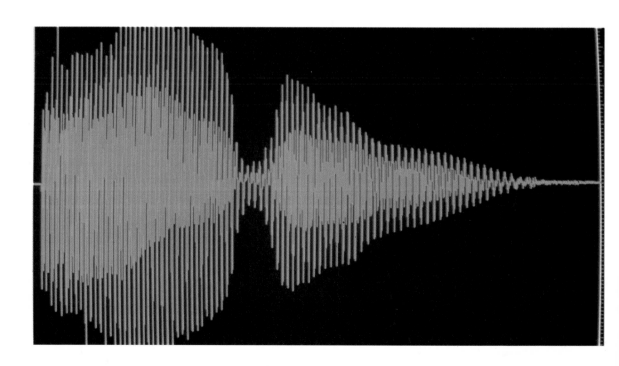

Scientists have made a special machine that can print a picture of your voice. When you speak, the machine changes the sound you make into lines that form a picture. Then the machine prints the picture on a piece of paper.

You can do many things with your voice to make it sound different. You can make it high or you can make it low. You can hold your nose or talk through a handkerchief. You can pretend that you're very old and make your voice shake. All of these things can make your voice picture look a little bit different.

The first voice that a baby learns to recognize is usually his mother's.

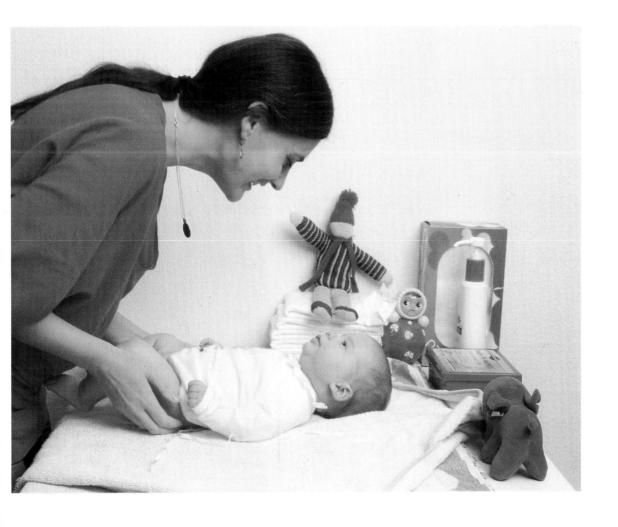

Your five senses

You can see, hear, touch, taste and smell. In other words, you have five senses. You see with your eyes and hear with your ears. Hands and feet help you to touch, your nose helps you to smell, and your tongue helps you to taste.

Your senses are all closely linked with tiny nerves which send messages to the brain about what you are experiencing.

At the back of the eye are nerves which carry messages to the brain about what you are **seeing**.

The little bumps on your tongue are called taste-buds, and inside are the **nerves** which tell your brain about what you are **tasting**.

There are many nerves inside your nose which tell you about what you are **smelling**.

Your skin is covered by millions of nerves. They tell your brain what you are **touching**.

Your ears turn sound into nerve messages, which tell your brain what you are **hearing**.

Your sense of sight

Your eyes and your brain work together to make you see.

When you look at something, the light that bounces off it enters your eyeball through a clear covering called the cornea. The light touches nerves at the back of your eye. The nerves send messages about the light to your brain. When your brain gets the messages, you know you're seeing something.

The coloured circle in your eye is the iris. In the centre of the iris is the pupil. The pupil looks like a black spot, but it is actually a hole that lets light into your eye.

Muscles in the iris make the pupil bigger or smaller to let in more or less light. When it is dark your pupil gets larger. In bright sunlight your pupil gets smaller. Behind the pupil is the lens. It is clear. Light passes through it.

The inside of your eye is filled with clear liquid that is a little like jelly. Light passes through that too. The light touches the back of your eye called the retina, where there are tiny nerves.

There are more than 100,000 nerves in your **retina**. Light touches the nerves and the nerves send messages about the light to your brain.

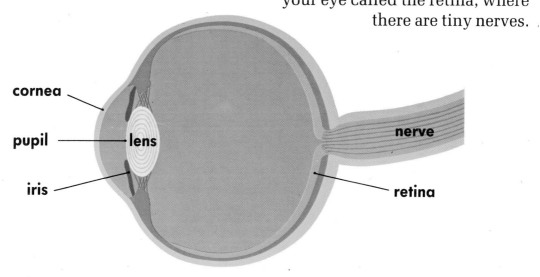

cornea

pupil — lens

iris

nerve

retina

These nerves send their messages to a big nerve. The messages travel along the big nerve to your brain. Your brain understands them, and tells you what you can see.

If your eyeballs were too long, you'd be **short-sighted**. So a far-off horse might look like this to you.

Seeing things well

If you look at something and can't see it clearly, your eyes need help.

Normal eyeballs are nearly round. People whose eyeballs are too long are short-sighted. They look at a far-off horse and they see only a blur. A clear picture of the horse does not form at the back of their eyes. Short-sighted people wear glasses to help them see things that are far away.

If you are short-sighted, pictures do not form on the back of your eye.

The lenses in a pair of **glasses** will put this right.

lens

With special glasses that help eyes to see far-off things, you'd see the horse clearly.

Contact lenses are smaller than the tip of your thumb.

People whose eyeballs are too short are long-sighted. When they look at something close to them, such as the words in this book, they see a blur. Long-sighted people wear glasses to help them see things that are nearby.

Some people wear contact lenses instead of glasses. Contact lenses are made of clear plastic. They are so small that they float on the tears that cover the eyes. The lenses fit over the irises and stay in place until the people who wear them take them out.

And if you are **long-sighted**, pictures do not form on the back of your eye.

A different shape of lens will put this right.

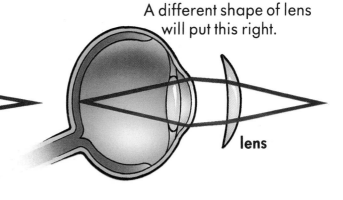

lens

Listen to this!

You hear sounds. People talk, dogs bark, there's music on the radio. You know about these sounds because your ears and brain work together.

Sounds are waves in the air. The sound waves go into your ear and bump against your ear-drum. Your ear-drum moves with the sound waves. When your ear-drum moves, it bumps into three tiny bones called the hammer, the anvil and the stirrup. As these bones bump against each other, the stirrup moves in and out of a place that looks like a snail's shell. This is called the cochlea.

Inside the cochlea are liquid and nerves. As the stirrup moves in and out of the opening in the cochlea, it makes waves in the liquid. The waves move across the nerves. When that happens the nerves carry messages to your brain. Your brain tells you there's a sound.

Most of your **ear** is inside your head. Your ear turns sounds into nerve messages. Nerves in your ear carry the messages to your brain. Your brain understands the messages and you hear sounds.

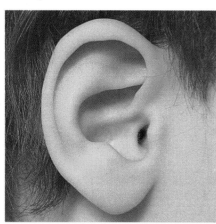

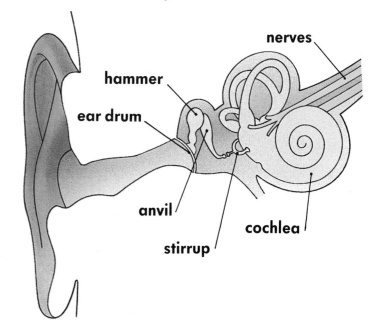

Humans can't move their
ears to hear small sounds,
but sometimes they can
put the sound close to
their ears!

These animals not only
hear better than us, they
can also move their ears
to catch small sounds.

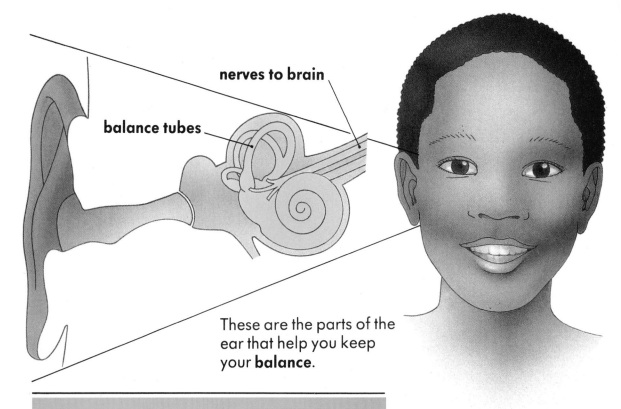

nerves to brain

balance tubes

These are the parts of the ear that help you keep your **balance**.

Keeping your balance

Your ears do more than help you hear. They have another important job – they help you to keep your balance.

They help you stay upright when you are moving and when you are standing still.

Inside your ear are three small hollow loops filled with liquid. These are your balance tubes. At the bottom of each loop are tiny cells that have hairs sticking out of them. Leading from each hair cell is a nerve.

When you move your head, the liquid in the loops moves across these hair cells. The nerves send messages to your brain. Then your brain sends messages to the muscles in your body. These messages help you keep your balance when you walk, run, skip or jump.

Whatever the position of the acrobat, messages from her ears will help to keep her perfectly balanced.

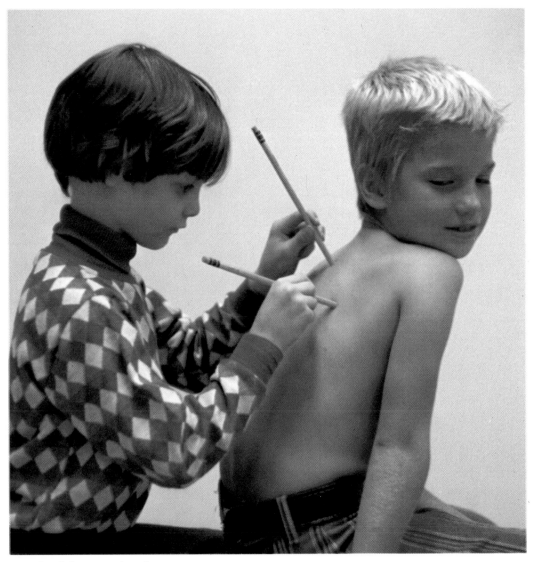

Put the blunt ends of two pencils on a friend's back. How far apart must they be before he can tell there are two pencils?

At your fingertips

A pin feels sharp. An apple feels smooth. Ice feels cold. A pillow feels soft. You know what all these things feel like because of nerves in your skin.

The nerves in your fingers are very close together. That's why your fingers are good feelers. Imagine you are ringing a bicycle bell

Some areas of your skin have more nerves than others. Just imagine if the nerves in the most sensitive places like your hands and feet were as widely spaced as those on your back — you'd look like this!

Different **nerve endings** tell you about different feelings.

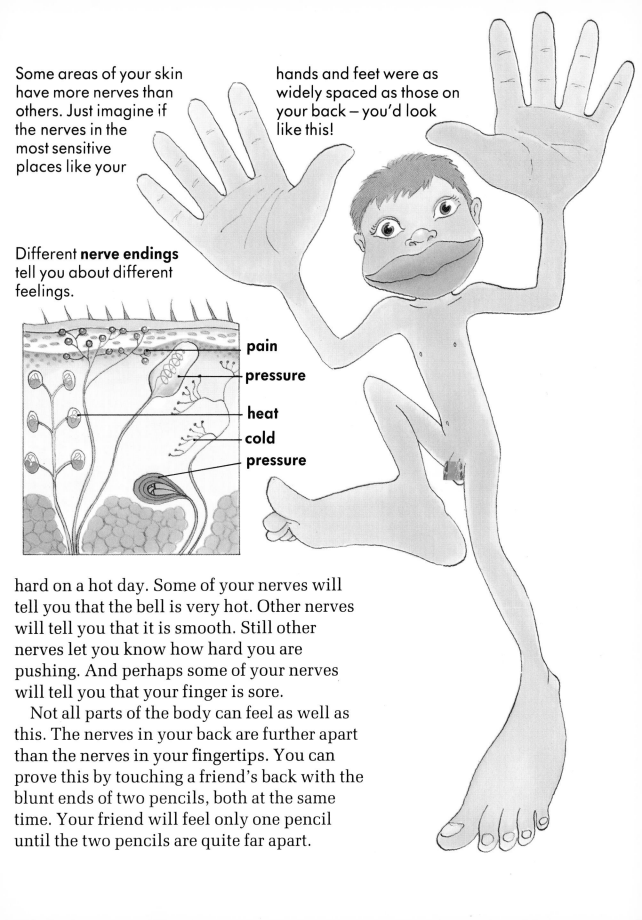

pain

pressure

heat

cold

pressure

hard on a hot day. Some of your nerves will tell you that the bell is very hot. Other nerves will tell you that it is smooth. Still other nerves let you know how hard you are pushing. And perhaps some of your nerves will tell you that your finger is sore.

Not all parts of the body can feel as well as this. The nerves in your back are further apart than the nerves in your fingertips. You can prove this by touching a friend's back with the blunt ends of two pencils, both at the same time. Your friend will feel only one pencil until the two pencils are quite far apart.

Inside your **nose** are nerves that pick up messages and send them to your brain. Your brain receives these messages and tells you what you are smelling.

Smells good!

Do you know what happens when you smell strawberries? Tiny bits that have broken away from the strawberries float in the air. These bits are called molecules. They are too small to see but your nose can find them.

Inside your nose there are lots of hair-like nerves. When the molecules enter your nostrils, the nerves send the message to your brain – and your brain tells you that you are smelling strawberries.

Your nose and your brain work together like this for every scent you smell.

Your sense of smell also helps your body to get ready to digest your food. When you smell something good to eat, your brain sends messages to your mouth and stomach. Your mouth waters and your stomach starts making juices before you even chew your first bite!

brain

nerves of smell

bone

inside of nose

nostril

bone

A snake uses its tongue to smell. It flicks its tongue out and waves it, picking up molecules in the air. Then it pulls its tongue back to a little hollow in the roof of its mouth. Nerves in this hollow then send messages to the snake's brain.

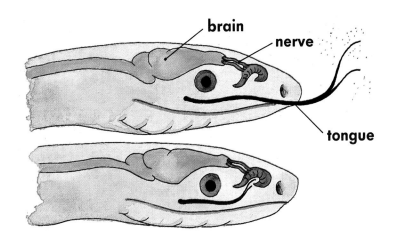

brain

nerve

tongue

It tastes good!

Yum! There's ice cream for dessert! But you have to eat your cabbage first. You know what you like and what you don't like because you are able to taste. Your tongue rolls each mouthful around your mouth. You taste your food as it tumbles over your tongue.

The tip, sides and back of your tongue are covered with little bumps. On the sides of

If you bite into a lemon, thinking it is an orange, your **tongue** soon tells you that you've made a mistake.

some of the bumps are tiny openings to your taste-buds. These are bud-shaped cells which are grouped together to look out for certain tastes. The taste-buds at the back of your tongue pick up bitter tastes, those at the sides of your tongue find salty tastes, and those at the very front of your tongue look out for sweet tastes. You can prove this by putting sugar, salt and lemon on different parts of your tongue. Inside the taste-buds are nerves that send messages to your brain. Your brain tells you what you're tasting.

The nerves in your lips, tongue, teeth and jaw muscles help you know what you're eating. They send messages to your brain about how hot or cold your food is, and whether it's rough or smooth, hard or soft.

Your food tastes better when you can smell it. When a cold stops up your nose, food doesn't taste as good. And food tastes better when you can see it too.

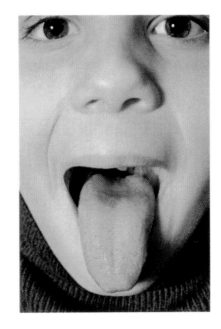

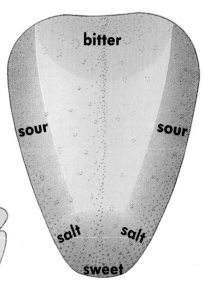

surface of tongue

taste bud

nerves

This is a single **taste bud**. Each one can only tell you about one kind of taste — bitter, sour, sweet or salt.

94

This boy has grown some of his adult **teeth**, but there are more waiting to grow through.

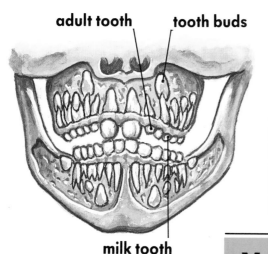

adult tooth   tooth buds

milk tooth

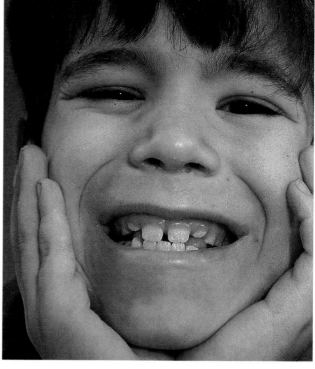

Your teeth

How old are your teeth? They're a little bit younger than the rest of you!

When you were a new-born baby no one could see the teeth in your mouth. They were just little tooth buds hidden deep down in your gums, waiting to grow. When you were between six months and one year old your baby teeth, or milk teeth, began to come through. When you were about three years old you had all twenty of your milk teeth.

When you were about six years old your adult teeth started to appear. One by one these adult, or permanent, teeth began to push your milk teeth out. When you are older you'll have thirty-two adult teeth. All the time your jaws will be growing to make room for them.

Stand in front of the mirror and look at your teeth. They don't all look the same, do they? This is because they have different jobs to do. The teeth at the front of your mouth are specially made for cutting your food. Now look at the pointed teeth next to them. These are teeth which have the job of gripping and tearing your food. At the back of your mouth there are flat, chewing teeth. Your teeth all work together to make sure your food is properly broken up into little pieces before you swallow.

This shows how many teeth you will have in your **upper jaw** when you've finished growing.

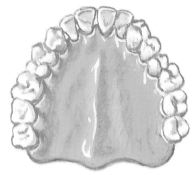

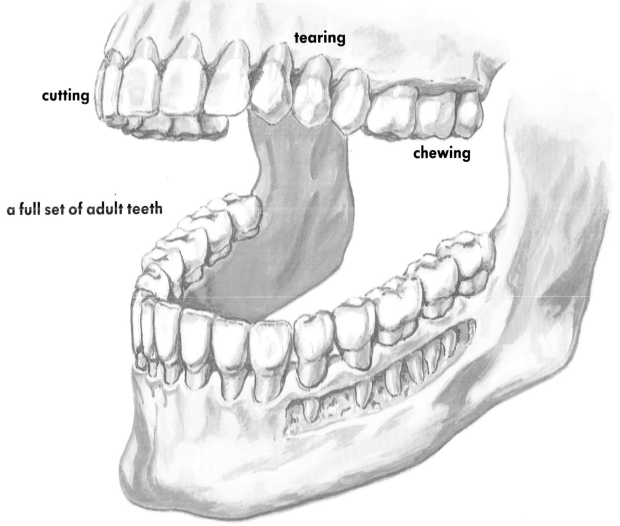

tearing

cutting

chewing

a full set of adult teeth

Plaque attack

Inside Jimmy's mouth, Captain Plaque and his army are waiting ....
"Not long now, boys. Let's hope he eats some nice sugary foods."

"Ho ho! Just right – boiled sweets. Get to work, boys."
Captain Plaque's Acid Army sets to work attacking the outside of Jimmy's teeth.
"Poison Patrol move to attack gums – now!"

"Go on, have some fizzy orange, Jimmy."
"Oh, all right. Thanks."

"And sweet orange drink. It gets better and better."
"Army Number 2 – on the double."
Captain Plaque calls out another army.

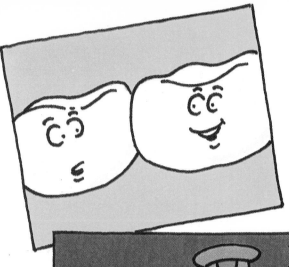

Meanwhile Jimmy's teeth are worried.
"I wish Jimmy would do something about this!"
"He will, I'm sure. He knows all about taking care of us."

"What a great afternoon. All we need now is a sticky bun."

At last something happens to stop Captain Plaque......
"I'll clean my teeth just like my dentist showed me. Round and round and up and down."

"Help! It's the toothbrush! Retreat, army. That Jimmy's too clever for us!"

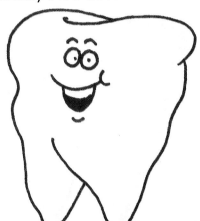

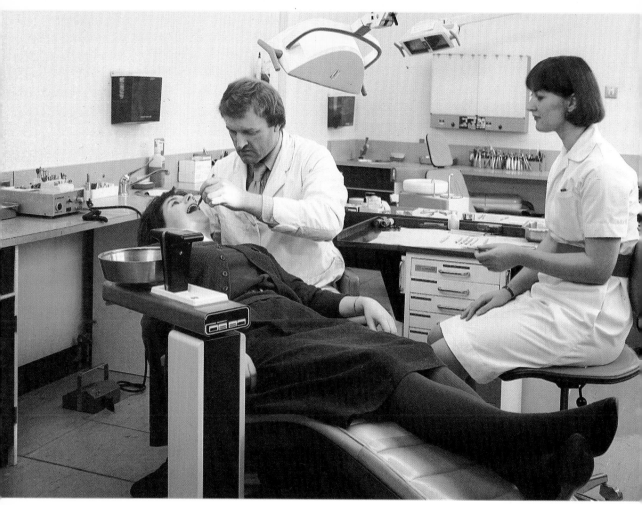

The **dentist** checks your teeth to make sure they are strong and healthy.

Visiting the dentist

Your dentist is your friend. Dentists are on your side in the battle against tooth disease and toothache. If you visit your dentist about twice a year you can help to stop any trouble in your mouth before it starts.

The first thing your dentist will do is ask you to sit in a special chair. It's a chair that moves so that it's easy to look into your mouth. Then your dentist will put a little round mirror on a handle into your mouth. This will help the dentist see the sides of your teeth. To feel for cavities, or holes, in your teeth dentists use tiny instruments called explorers. Your dentist will check all your teeth and call out to an assistant while working round your mouth. The assistant writes down notes about your teeth.

Dentists sometimes clean and polish your teeth to make them shine. They clear away all the left-over pieces of food you've missed with your toothbrush. They use noisy machines but, although these machines sound loud, they don't hurt.

Sometimes the dentist may find a little hole in one of your teeth which will need a filling. Sometimes you will be given an injection in the gums to deaden any pain while the dentist uses a drill. The drill makes a buzzing sound and stings a bit, but it cleans out the hole in your tooth. Then your dentist will mix up a paste. The hole is filled with this, and then rubbed and scraped to make it smooth. Now your tooth will be almost as good as new.

It's very hard for the dentist to work in your mouth, but you can help by opening your mouth wide and sitting still. Then it won't take the dentist long to finish the job. Your dentist will be pleased to show you the right way to brush your teeth. So if you aren't quite sure if you're doing it properly, just ask. Then you can carry on taking care of your teeth at home. Remember, the teeth that come through when you're only six have to last you a lifetime.

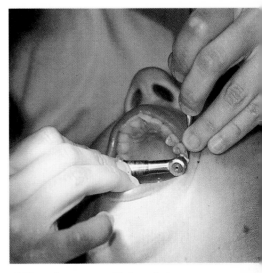

The dentist will finish his job more quickly if you can sit still and open your mouth really wide.

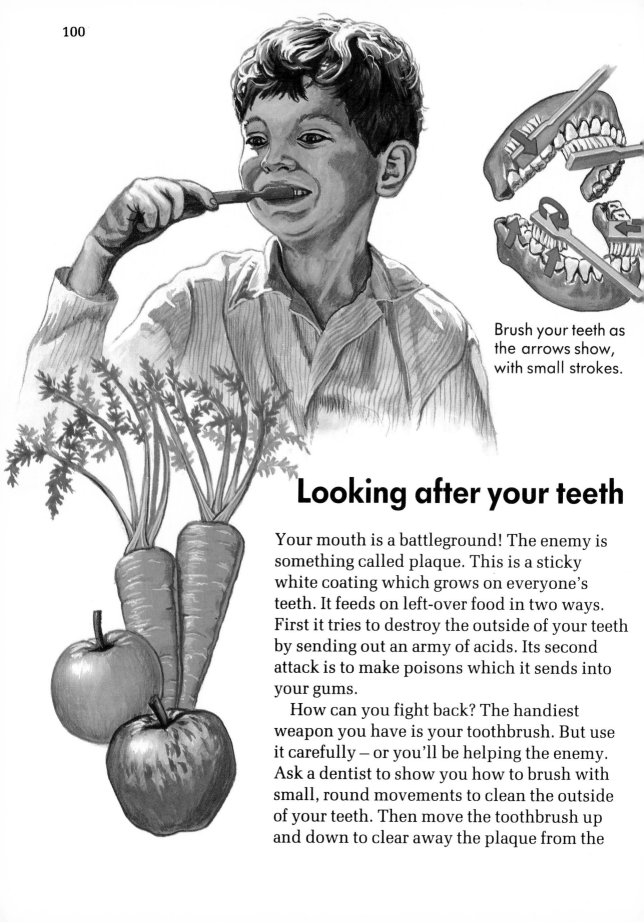

Brush your teeth as the arrows show, with small strokes.

Looking after your teeth

Your mouth is a battleground! The enemy is something called plaque. This is a sticky white coating which grows on everyone's teeth. It feeds on left-over food in two ways. First it tries to destroy the outside of your teeth by sending out an army of acids. Its second attack is to make poisons which it sends into your gums.

How can you fight back? The handiest weapon you have is your toothbrush. But use it carefully – or you'll be helping the enemy. Ask a dentist to show you how to brush with small, round movements to clean the outside of your teeth. Then move the toothbrush up and down to clear away the plaque from the

Plaque causes toothache by making a hole in the tooth, through to the centre.

Cutting teeth are called **incisors**.

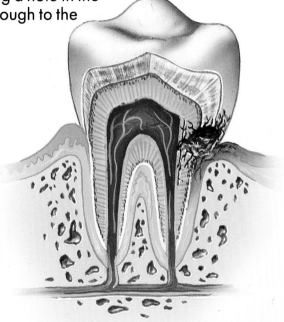

gaps in between your teeth. Don't brush backwards and forwards or you'll damage your gums. To keep back the enemy plaque, you'll need to clear the inside, outside and top of your big chewing teeth, and the inside and outside of your cutting teeth every day.

You can also help to win the battle by the food you eat. The more often you eat sweet things, the worse it is for your teeth. As soon as the plaque in your mouth knows something sweet is about, it sends out a new army of acids. The more times you eat something sweet in a day, the more acid armies you'll have to fight. So if you want to eat sweet things, try to eat them at mealtimes. Try to cut down sweet snacks and drinks between meals. Apples and raw carrots are best for teeth.

Chewing teeth are called **molars**.

Keep clean!

Look at your nails. Are they short and clean –
or long and dirty? And when was the last time
you washed your hands?

You might think these things aren't
important – that looking clean is just
something that adults worry about.
But keeping yourself clean is important if you
want to help your body keep free of germs.
Whether you've been playing, working,
shopping or visiting a friend, your hands will
pick up dirt from all around. If this gets on to
your food, it's easy to see how germs can travel
inside your body. It helps not to suck your
fingers or bite your nails too, because germs
can be carried to your mouth in this way.

The waste matter that comes out of your
body when you go to the toilet is full of germs
too, so it's important to wash your hands when
you've finished.

It's not just hands that get dirty. The skin on
other parts of your body picks up dirt too.
Also, when you are hot your body sweats.
Sweat is mostly water, which your body sends
out through tiny holes, called pores, in the
skin. If you don't wash this sweat off it dries
and becomes smelly. So it's important to wash
every day.

Another way germs get about is through the
drops of liquid you let out when you sneeze or
cough. You can help stop germs spreading by
covering your mouth and nose with your
hands or a tissue when you want to cough or
sneeze.

Animals can spread germs to your body too. Dogs and cats can pass on disease to humans, so don't let your dog lick your face and always wash your hands after you've been playing with animals.

Keeping your teeth and gums clean is important. You need to remove the harmful bits of food that get stuck in your mouth. People who don't look after their mouths by forgetting to clean their teeth can get bad teeth – and bad breath.

This might seem like a long list of things to remember, but keeping clean is easy really – because it makes you feel good. And a clean body is a healthy one.

I've got **mumps**.

I've got **chickenpox**.

Your body under attack

Have you ever had measles, German measles, chickenpox or mumps? These illnesses are often called childhood illnesses because most of us get them when we're children. Because they are illnesses most of us will have, it's helpful to know something about them.

When you get one of these illnesses, tiny germs called viruses attack your body. These germs travel from person to person in the drops of water you make when you sneeze or cough, or they are spread about in food and water. Viruses need to get into your blood before they can make you feel ill. They do this by sticking to your cells and then entering them. When they are inside your cells, they start to take over. But your body does fight back, and so these illnesses are usually not serious. After you've been ill special defence cells will recognize the virus if it tries to attack again and will destroy it as soon as it enters your body. So you'll probably get each of these illnesses only once in your whole life.

Measles feels a bit like a bad cold at first. But quite soon red blotches appear on your skin. This means the virus has just entered the cells under your skin and has begun to grow. As soon as this happens your cells start sending out signals to other parts of your body to get help. A fight is going on under your skin. The blotches you get all over your body are called a rash, and this usually takes about six

days to disappear. Sometimes, having measles makes you feel very cross and hot. The light might hurt your eyes. If you feel like this, it's a good idea to stay quietly in bed until you're better.

German measles doesn't make you feel quite so ill as ordinary measles, but you get a rash just the same. And you might feel some lumps behind your ears, which will mean that your glands are swollen. German measles doesn't last long – only a few days – and you might not even have to stay in bed at all.

Another virus that makes you spotty is chickenpox. The spots itch but you must be careful not to scratch them or you might let germs in and the marks won't go away. It helps if you keep your fingernails short, wear loose, light clothes in bed and take your mind off the spots by playing quiet games, reading or drawing. Let someone know if your spots itch a lot because the doctor might be able to give you some cream for them.

Mumps causes a swelling under your jaw-bone, giving you a puffy face. Sometimes it can be painful and you feel hot and miserable. If it hurts to swallow, ask for soft foods.

If any of these viruses makes you feel miserable, it might help to remember how many of us get them – and that you can have them only once! If you catch one, you'll need time away from school. If you have to stay in bed, try to be a happy patient – it's not much fun nursing a grumpy one!

I've got **measles**.

I've got a **cold**.

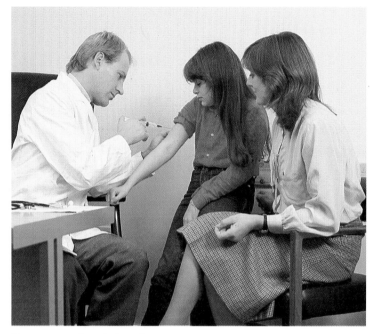

Doctors give **injections** to help you fight germs.

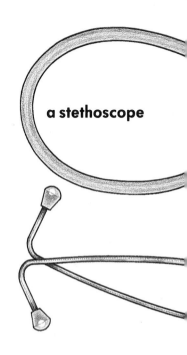

a stethoscope

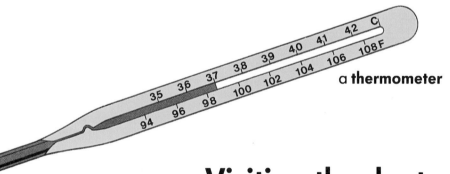

a **thermometer**

Visiting the doctor

You go to the doctor when you're ill. If you're very sick the doctor comes to see you at home. The doctor may give you medicine or an injection. Germs make you ill but the medicine helps fight the germs.

There are times when you go to the doctor and you're not ill at all. Sometimes a doctor will visit your whole class at school. This kind of visit is called a check-up.

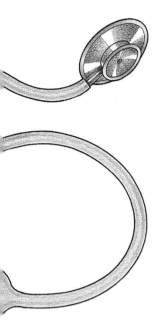

The thing around the doctor's neck is called a stethoscope. The ear-pieces fit inside the doctor's ears. Then she uses the stethoscope to listen to sounds inside your body. The doctor holds the stethoscope against your chest and listens to the sound of your heart beating.

Then the doctor moves the stethoscope around on your chest to hear your breathing.

There are sounds in your stomach, and she listens to these too.

Sounds tell a kind of story about what is going on inside you. Sounds help the doctor to know that you are growing up well and strong, exactly as you should.

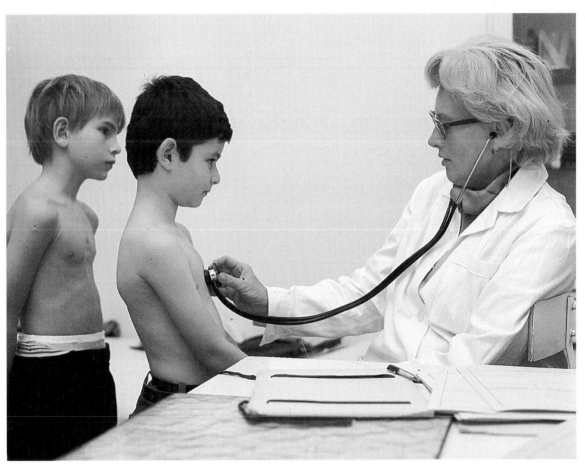

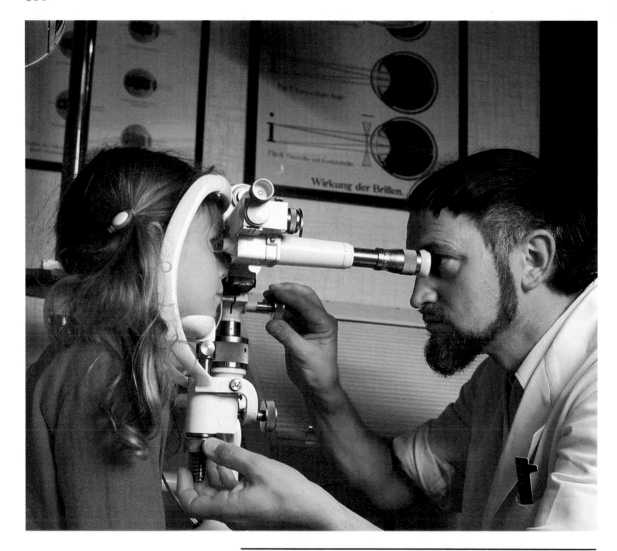

Inside story

Body sounds help tell the doctor a story about your health. But they are not the whole inside story. The doctor does other things too.

The doctor might shine a little light into your eyes. This light helps the doctor look into the inside of your eyes to see if they are healthy. Then he might ask you to read the letters on a wall chart. The doctor wants to be sure you are seeing as well as you should.

The doctor might shine another light into your ears. The light helps the doctor look into many of the inside places in your ears. He wants to be sure that all your ear openings are clear so that you can hear well.

Sometimes the doctor might talk to you about the kinds of food that are good for you. He might tell you to get plenty of sleep and to play outdoors a lot. You need food and sleep and fresh air to help you grow.

Doctors work with you to help keep your body healthy.

The doctor uses special instruments to look into your eyes and ears.

Emergency!

One day Ben had an accident. He broke his arm. He was taken to the emergency department of the hospital.

Nurses and doctors in the emergency room worked quickly. They didn't talk much to Ben, but he knew they weren't unfriendly. They were just very busy.

The doctors and nurses in an emergency department don't just help people who have broken bones. Sometimes people have swallowed something by mistake and the

Ben fell out of a tree and hurt himself. An ambulance came to take him to hospital.

doctors work fast to get it out. Other people have cuts and the doctors stop the bleeding. They take X-rays if they can't find out what's wrong because X-rays show pictures of our insides – the places we can't see.

Ben's X-ray showed a break in his arm bone. First the nurse put a bandage around Ben's arm. Then she put wet plaster over the bandage. The plaster dried into a cast that would keep Ben's arm still until it healed.

At last the doctor told Ben he could go home. Ben's mum and dad came to take him home. Ben said goodbye to the nurses and doctors, and thanked them for helping him.

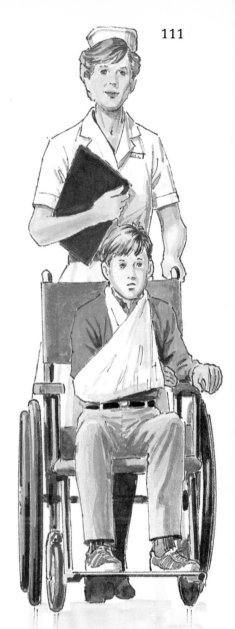

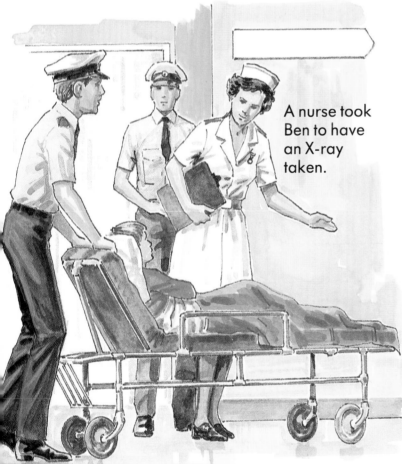

A nurse took Ben to have an X-ray taken.

The X-ray showed a break in his arm bone.

Going to hospital

Once, when Sara was ill, she had to go to hospital. She had to stay there for a while. Sara was taken there by her mother.

The hospital sounded different from Sara's house. There was a sound of wheels. There were meal trolleys, wheelchairs and beds on wheels.

The hospital smelt different from Sara's house too. It smelt of soap and floor polish, of medicine and flowers. It was very, very clean. People who work in hospitals must be clean too. Nurses and doctors wash their hands many times a day.

Sara and her mother walked a long way into the hospital. They walked past a lot of rooms called wards, with beds in them. When they got to the ward they had been looking for, the one where Sara would stay, Sara felt worried. She held her mother's hand tightly. Inside the ward they met a nurse. She smiled and said, "Hello, Sara," and Sara felt better. The nurse showed Sara to a bed with a screen round it and asked her to undress and get into bed. Sara changed into her pyjamas and got into bed. She felt a bit strange because it was the morning!

Sara and her mother looked at the bed. There was a card at the end with Sara's name on it. Sara and her mother talked and played games for a while, then Sara's mother had to leave. Sara felt a bit sad but the nurse said, "Come on, there's lots to do. And your mum will be back to see you later on."

Hospital doctors visit the patients regularly to make sure they get well quickly.

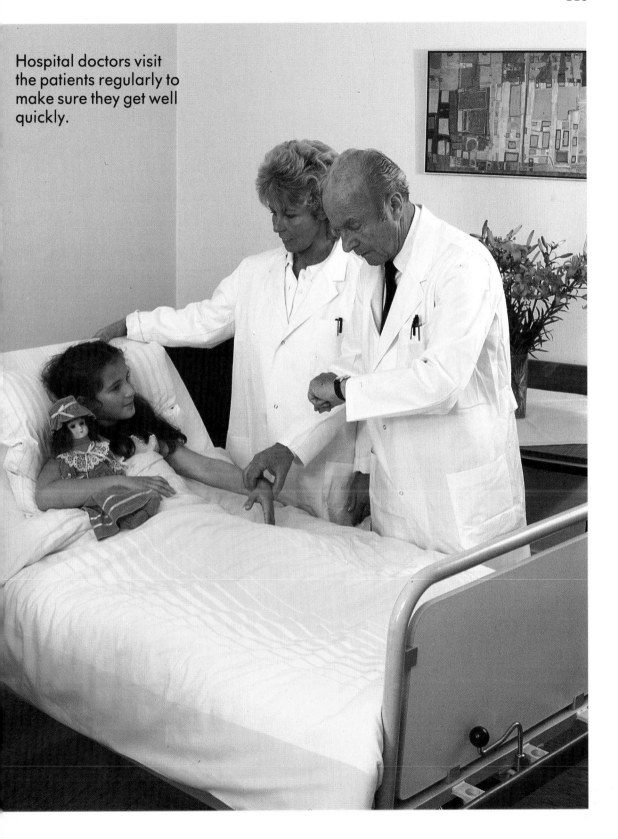

The children's ward

When Anne was in hospital she stayed in the children's ward. It was a long room with lots of beds, and there were other children in all the beds. Some of them smiled and waved to her.

There were lots of things for Anne to do. First of all she had a blood test. A nurse took a little blood from Anne. She used a needle – it did sting a bit, but it wasn't too bad. The nurse told Anne that the blood test would help the doctor know how to take care of her.

Then Anne was taken to a special room in the X-ray department. A nurse helped her to get up on to a table, and asked her to lie there without moving. A giant-sized camera took a photograph, called an X-ray, of Anne's insides. It didn't hurt at all.

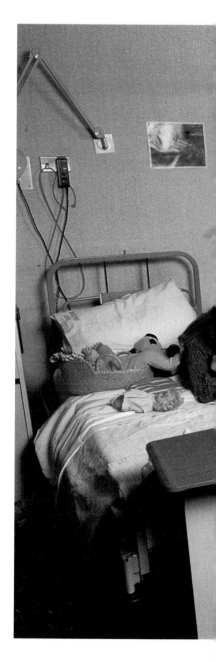

Back in the children's ward, another nurse took Anne's temperature with an instrument called a thermometer. The nurse wrote up some notes about Anne on the chart at the end of her bed.

After tea Anne watched television with the other children in the ward. Then her mother came to visit her. She brought Anne a new book to read and a jigsaw puzzle.

Anne stayed in hospital for a few days. She made some new friends there, and her mother came to visit her every day. A teacher came to the ward every day too, and she brought along something for all the children to do. In the afternoons Anne like to draw pictures with the other children. She even made a model.

The doctor came to see Anne every day. One day he told Anne she could go home. Her mother came to collect her, and Anne said goodbye to the other children and the nurses. She thanked them for looking after her so well.

In this **children's ward** the nurses try to make the children feel at home.

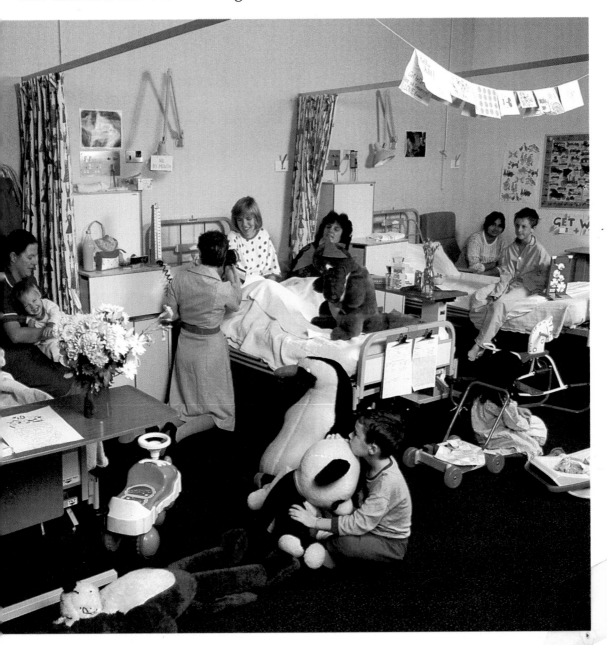

Before you were born

Where were you before you were born? You were warm and safe inside your mother's body, in a place under her stomach called the uterus or womb. But how did you get there? This is how it happened.

Inside your mother was a special kind of cell – an egg. It was smaller than a grain of salt, smaller than the tiniest dot you can make with your pencil.

Inside your father was another special cell called a sperm. It was smaller even than the egg, and it looked a bit like a tadpole.

To make you, your father's sperm cell travelled all the way from inside his body to inside your mother's body. Then his sperm cell met your mother's egg cell, and the two cells joined together to make one new cell. When that happened, a new life began. Your life.

sperm

egg cell

Many **sperm cells** try to join with the **egg cell**, but only one will get in.

The **new cell** divides into two.

The **two cells** divide into four.

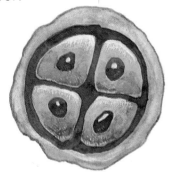

The dividing goes on and on.

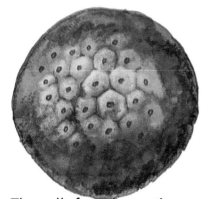

The cells form into a tiny baby. This special X-ray picture shows how the baby looks in its mother's womb several months before it is born.

Soon the cell began to divide. It divided into two cells. The two cells divided into four. The four cells divided into eight. The eight cells divided into sixteen cells. The tiny jelly-like cells stayed close together, and the dividing went on and on.

At first, all the cells seemed to be alike. But after a while each cell began to do its own job. Some cells became skin cells. Others became bone cells, heart cells, brain cells.

That is how you grew before you were born.

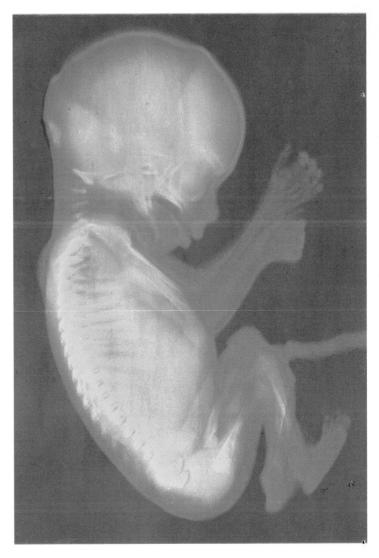

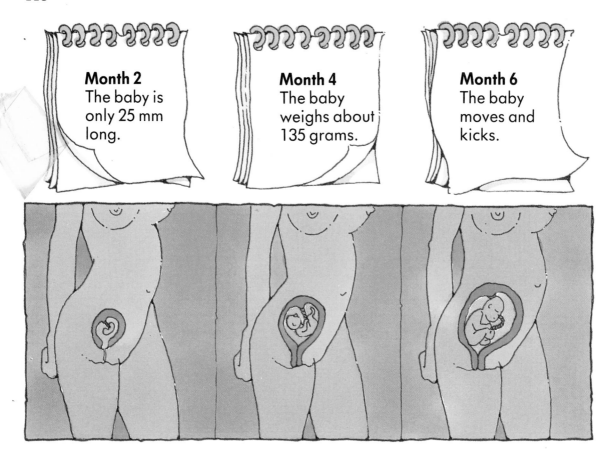

Month 2
The baby is only 25 mm long.

Month 4
The baby weighs about 135 grams.

Month 6
The baby moves and kicks.

Waiting to be born

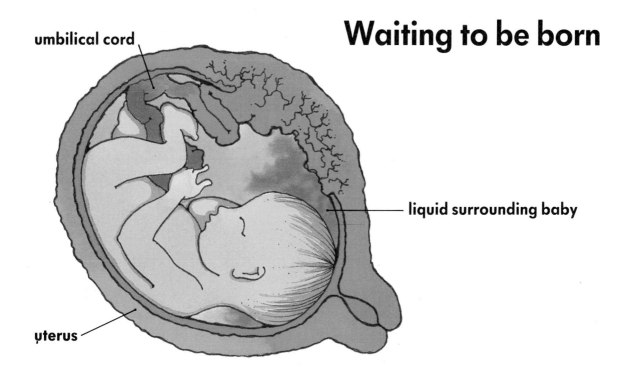

umbilical cord

liquid surrounding baby

uterus

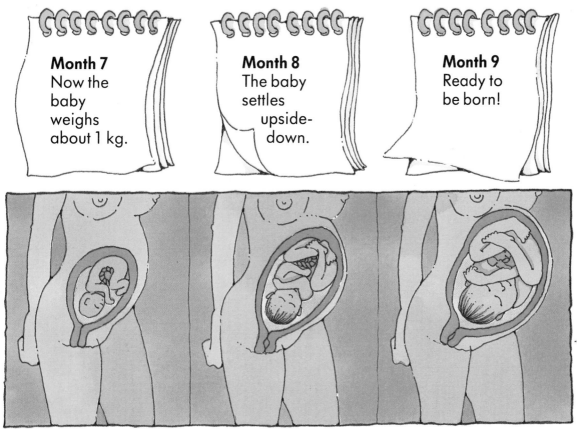

Month 7
Now the baby weighs about 1 kg.

Month 8
The baby settles upside-down.

Month 9
Ready to be born!

It took nine months for you to grow from a single cell to a baby. As you slowly grew, your mother's **uterus** became larger to make room for you.

You had a lot of growing to do before you were ready to be born. The egg and the sperm which had joined together needed a waiting place in which to grow. The waiting place was the uterus in your mother's body.

As you grew, your mother's uterus became larger to make room for you. You were safe and warm there, and you were fed through a cord called the umbilical cord that joined you to your mother. The place where this cord used to be is your tummy-button, or navel.

You began to move about. You waved your arms. You kicked your legs. Your mother could feel you moving and growing larger. For nine months you grew and changed shape.

Being born

When you were ready to be born, your mother felt a pushing inside her. The pushing stopped, then it started, then it stopped again. Each time, the pushing became stronger.

Your mother knew what the pushing meant. She knew it was a signal that you were ready to be born. The muscles of her uterus were pushing you out into the world.

The pushing got quicker and stronger. By now you were moving out of your mother's uterus and into her vagina, a stretchy tube leading from her uterus to an opening between her legs. Your mother helped you by pushing hard. At last your head pushed out of her body, through her vagina. And slowly the rest of you came out.

Most mothers go to hospital for their babies to be born, but sometimes they have their babies at home. In hospital there are doctors and nurses to help.

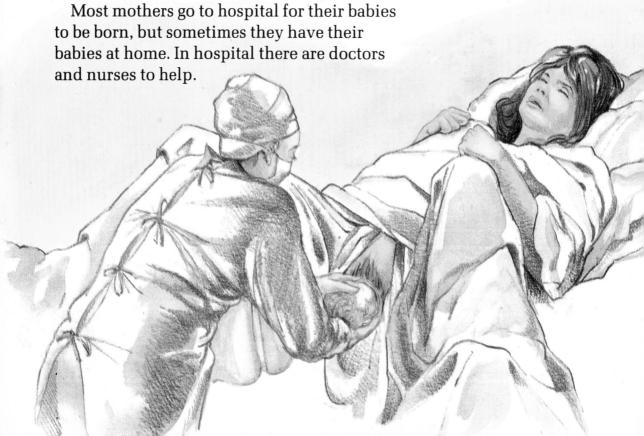

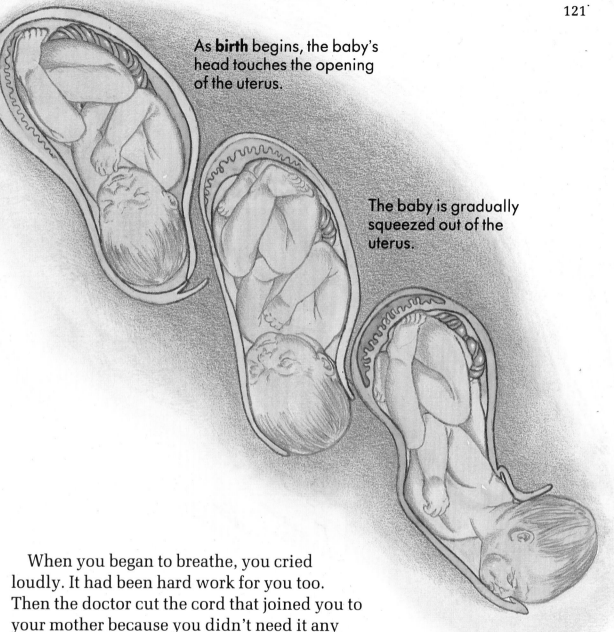

As **birth** begins, the baby's head touches the opening of the uterus.

The baby is gradually squeezed out of the uterus.

The uterus opens wide as the baby's head is pushed out.

When you began to breathe, you cried loudly. It had been hard work for you too. Then the doctor cut the cord that joined you to your mother because you didn't need it any more.

After that your mother rested. But lots of new things happened to you. You were carefully checked by the doctor or nurse to make sure you were healthy. The nurse weighed and measured you and gave you a bath. She dressed you in a nappy and a night-gown. Then she tucked you up to sleep because you were very, very tired.

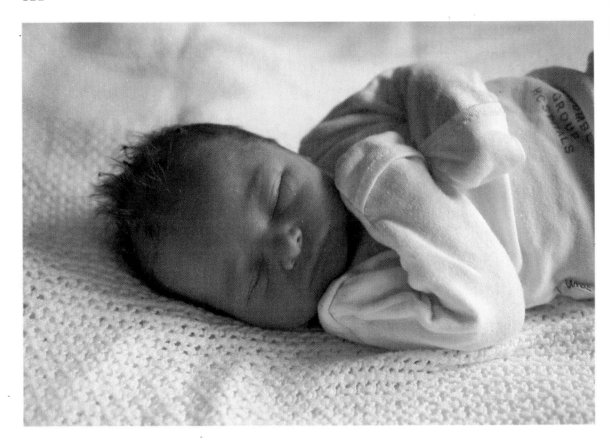

The new you

You're hungry, but you can't tell anyone – you can't speak. You'd like a cuddle but you can't go to find someone because you haven't yet learned how to walk, and your legs aren't strong enough. What do you do? You cry!

Most new-born babies cry a lot. Crying is the only way they can keep in touch with the people round them. For the first few months of your life, you couldn't do much at all. You cried and you ate and you slept.

After a while you stayed awake longer each day. You learned to like your bath. You liked to splash and kick in the water.

You grew. And you learned lots more things
– about yourself and about the world around
you. You learned to know your name.
You turned your head when you were called.
    You kept on growing and learning.
You gurgled when you were fed. You learned
to play with your fingers and to shake your
rattle. After a while you could sit up. Then you
could see all around. People stopped to look at
you in your pram. "That baby is growing up,"
they said.

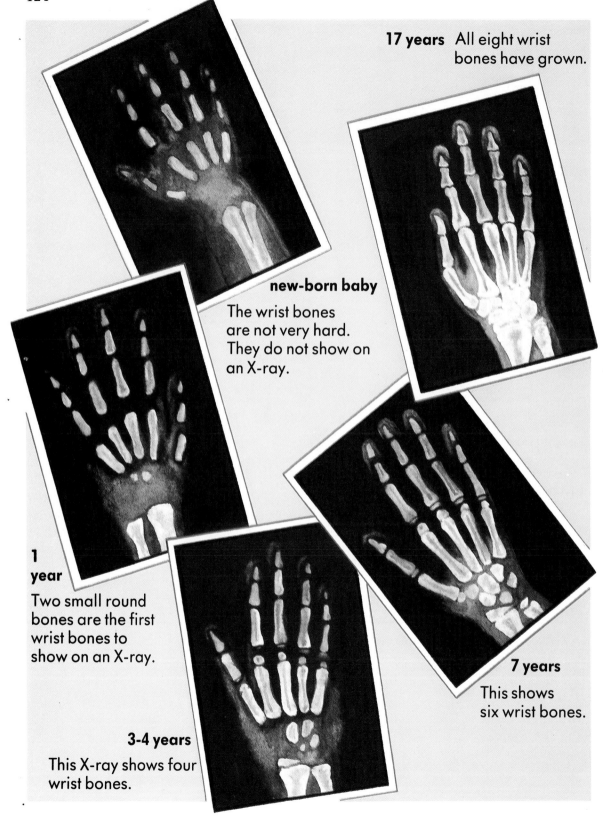

17 years All eight wrist bones have grown.

new-born baby

The wrist bones are not very hard. They do not show on an X-ray.

1 year

Two small round bones are the first wrist bones to show on an X-ray.

3-4 years

This X-ray shows four wrist bones.

7 years

This shows six wrist bones.

Growing bones

Have you ever held a small baby? Have you wondered why babies are much softer than you?

One reason babies are softer is because their bones have not hardened. When babies are born they have very few hard bones. Their skeletons are mostly made of a strong, slightly bendy material called cartilage. But bone cells work all the time, and so their bones get bigger and harder. Some will grow together.

Your bones are bigger and harder than a baby's, but they are not so hard as an adult's bones. They will keep growing and getting harder until you are about twenty-one.

If doctors want to check how children's bones are growing, they sometimes take X-rays of their wrists. Some children's wrist bones grow quickly, others grow more slowly. The important thing is that the bones are growing in a healthy, step-by-step way. If your wrist bones look right on the X-ray, then it is likely that all the other bones in your body are growing the way they should.

How tall will you be?

You are always growing. It is the easiest thing you do. It just happens. You can't see it happening. You don't seem to be much taller today than you were last year, yet the clothes you had last year are too small for you now. So you know you've grown.

How does it happen? There are more than ten million million cells in your body. Each cell keeps getting bigger and bigger. After a while each cell divides and becomes two cells. After more time the two cells divide and become four cells. The dividing of your cells goes on and on and on.

Each day your muscles have more cells in them. Your bones have more cells in them. So each day they grow a little bigger.

Why don't you go on growing and never stop? One reason is because, even though your

1 year

3 years

6 years

body makes new cells, other cells wear out.

A more important reason is to do with the tiny organs in your body called glands. You have tear glands, sweat glands, oil glands, glands that help you digest your food, glands that protect you from sickness, glands that make your heart beat faster. And you have glands that help you grow.

One gland, the pituitary gland, has charge over all other glands. It directs them so that they work together. These glands make things that cause you to grow or stop growing.

One day, somewhere between the ages of sixteen and twenty-three, your glands will tell your body to stop growing. Then you won't grow any taller.

By that time your legs will be about five times as long as they were when you were a baby. Your arms will be about four times as long. Your head will be about twice as big.

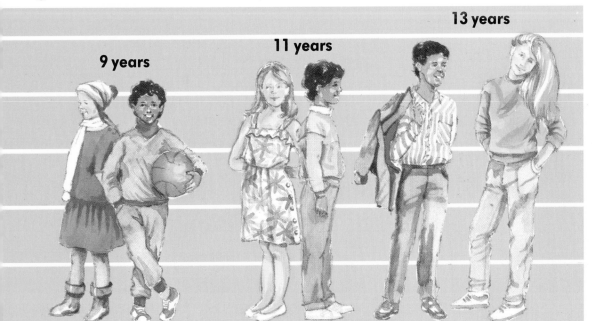

9 years   11 years   13 years

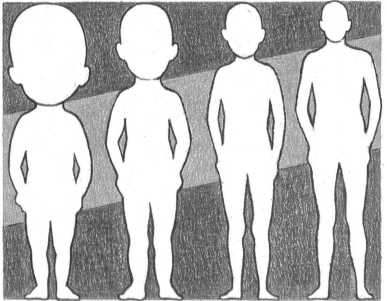

When you were born, your head made up about a quarter of your body's length. By the time you have finished **growing**, it will only make up about one eighth of your height.

Your body's changes

Grown-ups look different from children. They are bigger, of course, but they are different in other ways.

When girls are about twelve years old, their bodies begin to make the big change from children to adults. Their faces, the tops of their legs and their hips become more rounded. This is because there is a new layer of fat under the skin. Their breasts begin to develop, and hair begins to grow under their arms and between their legs.

Boys begin to change at about fourteen years old. Hair begins to grow on their cheeks, chin and between their legs. Their voices get deeper and their shoulders become wider. Their testes and penises get bigger. The testes are the two egg-shaped organs that make sperm cells. They are at the front of the body where the leg joins

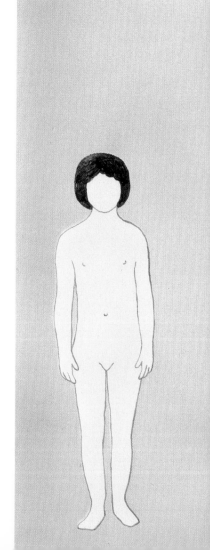

the body. The penis is the tube-shaped organ
in front of them.

These changes happen slowly over a few
years. When children's bodies have become
adults' bodies, they have grown all the parts
that they will need to make children of their
own. But having an adult body isn't enough –
our minds have to be grown-up too. Babies
need care and understanding and lots of time.
We must be very sure that we can give them
this before we decide to make them – we must
be sure that we are grown-up enough in our
minds as well as our bodies.

Over several years,
teenagers' bodies slowly
change shape. They are
no longer children – they
are now young adults.

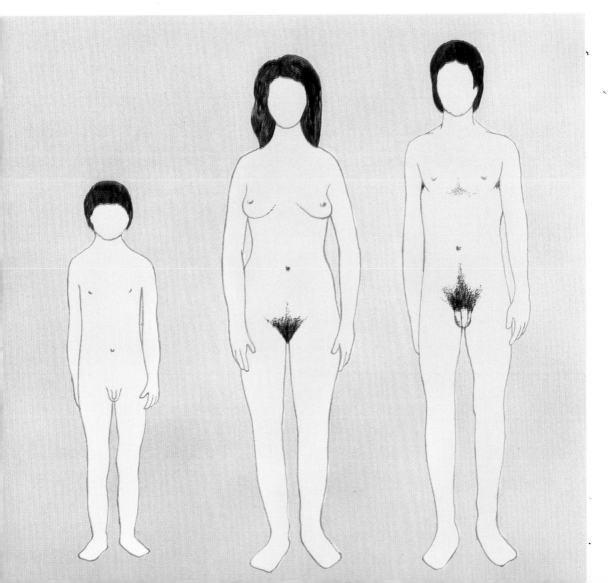

This baby's hair is the same colour as his mother's.

Who will you look like?

Do you ever wonder who you will look like when you grow up? Will you look like your father? Will you be as tall as he is? Will you look like your mother?

You will probably look a little like both your father and your mother. And you might look a little like your grandparents as well.

This is why. Something was passed along to you from both your parents in the egg cell and the sperm cell which joined to become you. In the egg cell and the sperm cell were tiny parts called genes. All genes have different jobs to do – some decide hair colour, some decide eye colour, some decide height. These genes carry all the information needed to form every part of your body. All together, the genes told your body how to grow into the special person that is you. Because some genes came from your mother and some from your father, you have a mixture of genes from both your parents. So you will look a little like both of them. Because your mother and father have genes which came from their parents, they look a bit like their own mother and father too. And these genes can be passed on to you.

All these genes put together in a certain way make you the person you are.

Hair and eye colour are decided by the **genes** you get from each of your parents. The gene for dark hair is called dominant because it overrules blond and red hair genes. Blond is dominant over red. The gene for brown eyes is dominant over blue.

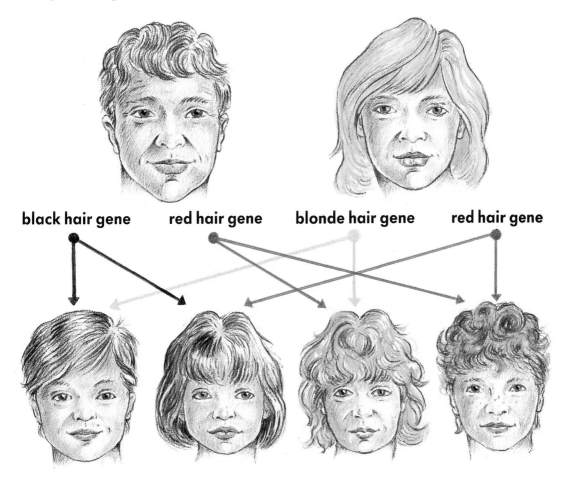

black hair gene   red hair gene   blonde hair gene   red hair gene

Your family

You may live with your natural parents – the mother and father you were born to. You are a family.

But perhaps you don't live with your natural parents. Perhaps you were adopted. If you were, your mother and father chose you to be part of their family. Or you might live with your mother and your stepfather, or your father and your stepmother. You might live just with your mum or your dad and be part of a one-parent family.

However it is, you are a family. There are many types of families but they all work in the same kind of way. The people in a family do a lot for each other. They stick up for each other, they are sad and glad with each other. They work and play together, and share things.

All around the world families are different. But no matter where they live, families do some things in the same way.

There are four **generations** in this large family group – great grandparents, grandparents, parents and children. Can you see two sets of twins?

134

A family tree

You can make a family tree of your own family. All you will need are some crayons or felt-pens, a pencil, paper and some photographs of the people in your family. If you don't have photographs, you can draw the faces yourself.

Start with a list of your relatives. First, you must put down yourself and your brothers and

sisters. Now add your two parents. Each of your parents has their own mother and father too – they are your grandparents.

Perhaps your parents have brothers or sisters? They are your uncles and aunts. If your uncles and aunts have children, they will be your cousins.

Now use your list to draw your own family tree. You can even put the pictures on different coloured squares to show which part of the family your relatives belong to.

cousin

cousin

aunt

uncle

grandmother

grandfather

When you started to crawl, your world got a little bigger.

At first, your mother's arms were all you knew.

The door opens

At first your world was small. It was only as big as your mother's arms. Then your bed and your room became part of your world.

Your world grew bigger. Soon your home and all things in it were part of your world. As you grew, your world grew. You began to take notice of more and more things around you. You tried to understand them.

Then you started to look outside. The things in your street seemed interesting. So did the

Learning to walk meant you could explore even more.

Now you're out in the wide world.

people. You watched them waiting for buses, washing cars and talking to each other. You saw them working – mending the roads, collecting rubbish, doing the shopping. Other people's houses looked interesting too. At the end of your road there were lots of other roads, all full of houses – but not quite like yours.

As you got older you began to notice other children. They were interesting. You watched them walking with their families, talking together and playing. And you wanted to play too. You wanted to become part of the big world outside your door.

The first day

Going to school on the first day of the new school year is always exciting.

You might wake up early in the morning. Perhaps you don't feel like eating much breakfast. You don't want to be late.

Lots of questions race through your mind. What will your new teacher be like? What will your new room be like? Where will you sit? What new books will you have? They will be more grown-up than last year's books.

Perhaps you haven't seen some of your friends all summer. There will be lots to talk about. And there might be new children in the classroom – new friends.

It will all be strange at first. But you know that soon everything will be friendly and familiar. Soon you'll learn together and do things together.

The first time you went to school you were probably a bit scared. You didn't know what to expect. You may have been shy with so many children all around you. But you soon got used to it. You liked being with the other children, you learned things and you made friends.

Every new term is a little bit like that first time, but now you know there's a lot to look forward to!

Asking questions and finding answers

As you grow, you think and wonder all day long. You think of questions and you try to find the answers. You might wonder how your dog knows you're home from school even before you open the door. Or why it doesn't hurt to cut your hair or your nails. You might wonder too why you yawn.

You try to find the answers to these questions by using your eyes, or by reading books, or by asking people. Then you find out that dogs have extra-sharp hearing and can tell one set of footsteps from another. So your dog·

knows you by your footsteps. And that cutting your hair and nails doesn't hurt because there are no nerves in those places, and you feel pain only in the parts of your body where there are nerves. And you find out that you yawn because you're tired. The great gulps of air you take in as you yawn bring extra oxygen into your body and make you feel more wide awake.

You understand the answers to these questions – and thousands of others – because you have a mind.

You wonder about all kinds of things. You might wonder why you were made. What does being alive mean? And how do you know what is right or wrong? You might ask your mother or father, a relative or a friend – someone you can talk to. You could try to find the answers together.

You know they're your best **friends** when you trust them with a secret.

Friends

Who do you share a secret with? Who do you tell your favourite joke to? Who do you call for when you want to play? Your best friend.

Most of us have a best friend, but we have lots of other friends too. Friends can be your own age – or they might be older or younger than you.

Friends are people you know well and feel safe with. But you don't feel safe with everyone. Because your parents have told you that not everyone is a friend, it's good to have people you are sure of. This is why friends are important. You can trust your friends.

Sometimes your friends make you cross, but you usually don't stay angry for long because you know that your friends didn't mean to hurt you.

Think of all the things that you like about your friends. You might like one friend because he is fun to be with. Another of your friends might be good at listening when you want to talk to someone. All your friends will have something special that you like them for. And don't forget that you are a friend to them too!

Friends will always listen when you've got a good joke to tell.

144

It takes a **special skill** to join in this game of football.

Everyone is special

Think of the people you know at school and in your neighbourhood. They are all very different. There are probably some who can't do all the things that you do – or some that can do things you can't.

This is just another way in which everybody in the world is different. Just as no one in the world looks exactly the same as you, no one else in the world can do exactly the same things as you. One person might be able to draw a picture of anything, but couldn't write a good story – or remember a joke! And someone who is brilliant at sports might be hopeless at maths. If there are some things that you're not very good at, there's always something else that you can do well.

This is true about everyone – especially if someone has a part of their body that doesn't work properly. Being able to get about easily, or see and hear things clearly is only one of the things that people are able to do. And whenever something goes wrong, the body has a way of balancing things up. If one sense doesn't work, the others become super-sharp. For example, blind people can often hear and feel things that people who can see don't even notice. But when we think about the things we can't do, it's really important to remember that's only one small part of us. It's the things that we can do, that make each of us a special person.

This boy has a different hobby – he's developing his skill at programming a personal computer.

Feelings

As you grow, your face doesn't change much. It gets a bit bigger and thinner, but you still always look like you.

Your fingerprints don't change at all. But one part of you that does change from hour to hour and day to day is your feelings. You can be happy, sad, excited, quiet, cross, friendly, shy, scared or brave. One minute you might feel very grown-up. The next minute you might surprise yourself by acting younger than you are. It's all part of growing up – and it seems a muddle sometimes.

Feeling cross is not a nice feeling. It makes you upset inside. You can feel angry over lots of things. Your friend might make you cross if he doesn't play fairly, adults might make you angry by asking you to do something you don't like. Then it's easy to shout and make a fuss. The worst thing about being cross is that afterwards you often wish you hadn't acted like that, but you just can't seem to help it.

As you grow up you learn about your feelings. You can understand them better, and this helps you. But when you're young all your different feelings can muddle you. Perhaps it helps then to know that sometimes everyone feels the same.

It feels very sad to think that you will never see your pet again.

Losing someone you love

Have you ever had a pet that has died? It hurts, doesn't it? It doesn't hurt like your leg hurts when you've fallen over. It's a different kind of pain. It makes you feel sad.

For you, the death of your pet means that you won't ever see it again. But it's not just pets that die, sometimes people die. People you love. This means that you won't ever see them again. It hurts a lot.

Death is a fact of life. It happens to everyone one day. But for the people whose friends or relatives die, it's very hard. They are left missing the dead person. They feel lonely and strange and sad.

When someone gets very old, all the things that their body could do begin to happen more slowly. At last, like an old, worn-out machine, their body stops and they die. But it's not just old people who die. Sometimes children and babies die, or young mothers and fathers. Then it's very hard to understand. Perhaps their bodies were not working properly, or they might have been in an accident and were killed.

Whoever has died, in whatever way, it's very hard for the people who love them. They may become very quiet and want to be on their own for a long, long time. Other people may get very angry, and this anger goes on for a long time too. They may feel angry at everyone, they may even be angry at the person who has died for leaving them. This quietness or anger after someone has died is called grieving. It means that people are trying to understand and accept the death of someone they love in their own special way.

Many people don't like to talk about death. They say it's a sad subject. You don't need to think about it often, but it's important to sometimes. This will help you when you meet with death in your own life. It's important to know about grieving so you can try to understand the way people act when someone they love has died. Also, if someone you love dies, it's important to know that your feelings of quietness or anger are normal, and that they will go away in time.

Remember too that it would be a very sad thing if there was nobody left behind who cared. The hurt you feel is part of the caring. Because of this you should never want there to be no pain. And you should never pretend it isn't there.

Pets and people never leave you completely. They stay with you in your memories. In this way they are part of you for ever.

You may feel very sad or even angry when someone you love has died. As time passes, your sadness will not hurt so much.

Looking after yourself

All the pages in this book show you how special your body is. It is like a machine and it needs to be looked after carefully to keep it in good condition.

Exercise is an important way to keep your body healthy. Walking, running, swimming, cycling and jumping are all good for your heart and muscles. If you exercise while you are young and growing you can help make sure your body works as it should. Your muscles will develop if you use them and strong muscles will help the shape of your bones. Exercise also helps you to breathe properly, and makes blood move quickly through your body. You feel warm and good. When you get older, exercising helps you to stay healthy.

Making sure you get enough sleep is important for your body too. When you sleep many of your muscles rest – even though you change position about forty times a night! But it is the brain that needs sleep the most. To help scientists find out about sleep, some people have stayed awake for two or three days and nights. Then the scientists tested them. The tests showed that their muscles worked quite well without sleep, but that their tired brains made them muddled.

Not everyone needs the same amount of sleep, but don't forget how important it is to have the right amount for you. When you are too busy playing or watching television to want to go to bed, try to remember how much your brain needs its rest.

Scrapbook

Here are some projects, all about you, that you might like to do for fun.

You can put the poster on your bedroom wall or keep it in a safe place.

A poster of yourself

You will need:

lots of sheets of paper
sticky tape
crayons, felt-pens
a friend

Lay the sheets of paper on the floor and tape them together until you make one whole sheet, just a bit taller than you. You might need to lie down on top of the paper to check this. Ask your friend for help.

Now take off your shoes and lie down on the big sheet of paper. Ask your friend to draw around you with a crayon or a felt-pen.

Cover the outline with all the information about yourself you think is important – likes and dislikes, colour of hair, eyes, age, name, friends, hobbies.

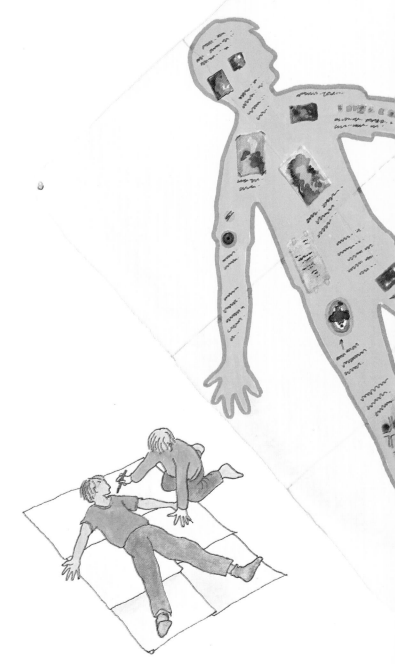

All About Me book

This is a cross between a scrapbook and a diary. An exercise book will do, or one of the big scrapbooks you can buy in the shops. Fill it with all kinds of bits and pieces that are special to you – old birthday cards, snapshots, letters, holiday postcards, as well as any notes you want to make about things that have happened to you.

It makes a useful record, to show you the many ways you change as your body grows.

Index

This index is an alphabetical list of the important words and topics in this book.

When you are looking for a special piece of information, you can look for the word in the list and it will tell you which pages to look at.

If you do not find what you want in this index, you can look at the General Index in Volume 16. This gives a list for all the books in **Childcraft**.

Acknowledgement

The publishers of **Childcraft** gratefully acknowledge the following artists, photographers, publishers, agencies and corporations for illustrations used in this volume. All illustrations are the exclusive property of the publishers of **Childcraft** unless names are marked with an asterisk *.

6–7	Zefa Picture Library*
8–9	Joanna Stubbs (B.L. Kearley Ltd)
10–11	Roy King (Specs Art Agency)
12–13	Kirsty McLaren; K.J.N. Fabby (Zefa Picture Library*); Childcraft diagram
14–15	Product Illustration, Inc; Childcraft photo by Joel Cole, Rush-Presbyterian St Luke's Medical Center, Chicago; Kotch (Zefa Picture Library*)
16–17	Annabel Milne
18–19	Annabel Milne; N. Schaefer (Zefa Picture Library*); Phoebe Dunn*
20–21	Nicholas Devore (Bruce Coleman Ltd*); Damm, Leidmann, Dr M. Beisert, Warren Williams, Hoffmann-Burchardi (Zefa Picture Library*)
22–23	Nicholas Berry (Specs Art Agency); Childcraft staff art
24–25	Annabel Milne; Childcraft diagram
26–27	Claire Smith
28–29	Childcraft diagram
30–31	Zefa Picture Library*
32–33	Childcraft diagram; Zefa Picture Library*; Gary Slater (Specs Art Agency)
34–35	The Wright Bros (Specs Art Agency)
36–37	Annabel Milne; Childcraft diagrams
38–39	Annabel Milne; Kirsty McLaren
40–41	Malcolm Livingstone
42–43	Kirsty McLaren
44–45	Childcraft diagram; The Wright Bros (Specs Art Agency)
46–47	Tony Herbert (B.L. Kearley Ltd)
48–49	Nigel Alexander (Specs Art Agency)
50–51	The Wright Bros (Specs Art Agency); Childcraft diagram
52–53	David Mostyn
54–55	Malcolm Livingstone
56–57	Nigel Alexander (Specs Art Agency)
58–63	Diana Leadbetter (Young Artists)
64–65	Kirsty McLaren
66–67	Michael Strand (B.L. Kearley Ltd)
68–69	Tony Herbert (B.L. Kearley Ltd)
70–71	Childcraft diagram; Gary Slater (Specs Art Agency)
72–73	Kirsty McLaren; Nigel Alexander (Specs Art Agency)
74–75	Leidmann (Zefa Picture Library*); Gary Slater (Specs Art Agency)
76–77	N. Schaefer (Zefa Picture Library*); Hank Morgan (Science Photo Library*)
78–79	Hugel/Fr, Armstrong, Sammer, J. Plaff (Zefa Picture Library*)
80–81	Childcraft photo; Childcraft diagrams; M. Schneider (Zefa Picture Library*)
82–83	The Wright Bros (Specs Art Agency); Childcraft photos by Ed Reif
84–85	Childcraft photo; Annabel Milne; Mick Loates (Linden Artists Ltd); Kirsty McLaren
86–87	Annabel Milne; Kurt Scholz (Zefa Picture Library*)
88–89	Childcraft photo; Malcolm Livingstone
90–91	Kirsty McLaren; Duncan Harper
92–93	Childcraft photos; Annabel Milne